MANAGING PEOPLE AND PROBLEMS

Managing People and Problems

Quentin de la Bedoyere

WILDWOOD HOUSE

First published in hardback 1988 by
Gower Publishing Company Limited

This paperback edition published 1989 by
Wildwood House Limited
Gower House,
Croft Road,
Aldershot,
Hampshire   GU11 3HR
England

Gower Publishing Company
Old Post Road,
Brookfield,
Vermont 05036,
U.S.A.

British Library Cataloguing in Publication Data
de la Bedoyere, Quentin.
   Managing people and problems.
   1. Personal management.
   I. Title
   658.3   HF5549

Library of Congress Cataloguing in Publication Data
de la Bedoyere, Quentin.
   Managing people and problems.
   Bibliography:P.
   1. Personnel management. 2. Problem solving.
   I. Title.
   HF5549.D395   1989   658.3   87-25548

ISBN   0-7045-0625-4

Printed and bound in Great Britain at
The Camelot Press plc, Southampton

Contents

Preface

This book will tell you how to manage problems face to face. Not just 'personnel' problems, but the whole variety of problems which involve people. It demonstrates a framework which has been tested and found effective in actual management situations, and it describes the skills which are needed to put it into action.

The successful manager of the 1990s will need one skill above all others – the skill of managing people. He can spend months and years of his time studying the techniques of business from market analysis to computers and, at the end, he will be a technician. But if he has learnt how to manage people he can run a successful business, and hire all the technicians he needs. Solving problems face to face is one of the key skills for the management of people.

The book reflects two philosophies. The first is that the good manager wants to develop good subordinates – people who will contribute efficiently and responsibly to the business enterprise, and enjoy themselves while doing so. The second is that good intentions are no substitute for the action that gets results. This is not a book of theory, but a book of practice.

It is built around the LEGUP framework – Listening, Exploration, Goal setting, Underpinning and Pursuing. Each stage of this problem solving system has its relevant skills, and these are demonstrated using concrete examples – mostly taken from real life. A final chapter describes the use of the method for general management tasks, for working with the boss and for working with small groups. The reader is taught

how to practise all aspects of the method since practice is
necessary for the mastery of any skill.

The book has been written for all managers from the
junior supervisor in his first post to the chairman of the
international megacompany. The budgets may be bigger,
but the skills are the same. Indeed the supervisor who knows
how to solve problems face to face is set to become chairman
one day. It is particularly relevant to the man or woman who
manages his own business, where the efficient solving of
problems is critical to success or failure.

How I came to write this book

I first decided that I had better learn how to solve problems
efficiently when I was working voluntarily as a counsellor for
the Catholic Marriage Advisory Council (CMAC). My
clients presented a variety of problems, often desperate,
which covered the span of human experience. They appreci-
ated my listening ear and my sympathy, but what they
wanted was their problems solved. And I wanted to solve
their problems too; I had a long waiting list. Just at that time
– it was a number of years ago – CMAC had begun to
introduce systematic problem solving methods, drawing particularly on the work of Gerard Egan (see bibliography) of
Loyola University, Chicago. The methods I was learning
actually worked. I believed I was becoming what Egan described as an 'effective helper'.

Back at Sun Life of Canada the problems were, for the
most part, rather different – just the everyday problems of a
working manager in a business with rather high standards.
But I soon found that I was incorporating my new skills into
my professional life, and that they were proving equally
effective. As time passed I gradually modified the methods,
simplifying them and adapting them to the particular
demands of the business environment. I hope, and think, I
remained faithful to the principles. It seemed to me that
methods and skills tested in two organizations – one dedi-
cated to financial security and the other to emotional
security – must be worth sharing with other managers.

Acknowledgements

My debt to the CMAC, to Sun Life of Canada and to Gerry Egan, is obvious from what I have written. But I owe a more particular debt to my wife, Irene. She brought her long and expert counselling experience to my aid, made major contributions to the planning of the book, and reviewed the text in detail – making many suggestions which I have incorporated. I cannot hold her responsible for the faults of the book, but she has a large share in any virtues it may possess.

Finally, my thanks are due to Methuen for permission to quote from the Calman cartoon referred to in Chapter 7.

Quentin de la Bedoyere

1 People and Problems

The ability to solve problems is the measure of a manager, and problems are a constant feature of his work. He needs not only to find a correct solution but to find the one solution which will succeed because it takes into account the human factors involved. It has always been important for managers to be successful problem solvers, but never more important than today. Unfortunately people are not naturally good at the task because they do not employ a systematic method for tackling it. However, such methods have been established; and they can be used effectively by managers who are ready to practise the skills involved.

A manager is in business to solve problems; and the measure of his worth is how good he is at doing it. Just as we would have no doctors without illness, or policemen without crime, we would have no managers without the problems which are the daily stuff of business. Some may be big, many are small, but they come at us from every angle demanding that we solve them quickly and effectively. Look back for a moment at your last working day – starting when you arrived at your desk – and list the problems which required your attention. You may be surprised at the number and the variety. If I carry out that exercise for the day I'm writing this, the list is formidable:

- Ensuring that a staff member, who had miscalculated some key market share figures, facsimiles a correct

1

version to New York at the beginning of their working day. Expressing displeasure to staff member for carelessness – without demotivating him.

- Convincing Management Services Department that the new computer equipment I need falls within company purchasing criteria.

- Deciding whether to divert some budget earmarked for educational sponsorship to paying for a new corporate brochure.

- Dealing with an incident where a colleague has been trying to poach a valued member of my staff – quick action required with staff member and colleague.

- Persuading a product management team that they will have time to complete a complex cost benefit study in time for me to present it at a meeting next week.

And that list only takes me to eleven o'clock. I will spare you the rest of what was a quite typical day. Your list may not be identical but it will be just as long; and just as challenging to your managerial skills. It will also share a common characteristic with my list – most, perhaps all, of the problems have to do with people. Even the decision about my publicity budget, which seems at first sight merely to be about financial resources, is really about people. How are Personnel going to feel about losing the educational sponsorship which they see as a good way to recruit among the brighter school-leavers? What will be the reaction of the Sales Department if I have to tell them that the brochure they see as an important promotional aid will not materialize this year?

I remember well a piece of advice I received from my boss when I took my first appointment as a young trainee manager. He said: 'Up till now you've been a salesman and your success has depended on your own achievements. From now on it's going to be quite different – your success will depend on other people's achievements.' It was good advice, and it stuck. Management is about people and people present problems.

Practical problem solving

This book has been written to help you to become a better problem solver. You may, of course, be good at it already; and if you are then you will know that it is a skill which needs continual revision and practice in order to maintain standards, let alone improve. But if you know in your heart of hearts that your problem solving skills are at best patchy then you will be looking for a sensible way to develop them. You don't want gimmicks; you are suspicious of short cuts or magic remedies; you want methods which have been proved in practice.

Here are some examples of the kind of problem which managers ordinarily meet, and with which this book will be concerned.

Victoria was asked two months ago to produce a report on possible locations for building a new plant in Belgium. Although you have spoken to her about this several times she doesn't seem to be making much progress. On the last occasion she gave as her reason that pressure of administrative work was delaying her from getting down to the task.

Dave, a bright young man who joined you a year ago, is someone you would like to promote to his first supervisory position. But he has shown no signs of ambition, and may be someone who would prefer to stay with the 'lads'.

You have been approached by a valued manager who is within a few years of retirement. She tells you that for some time she has lost her zest for work and feels that, in fairness to the company, she should retire now.

You have noticed that a junior manager has been authorizing an unusually large amount of overtime payments for staff. You cannot see immediately what the reason for this might be; and it's throwing your budget out.

Prendergast, a successful sales manager, has asked for an interview to discuss salary. Your records tell you that his bonus, which is related to his team's performance, has dropped over the last quarter.

Recently your boss has reversed some of your decisions, speaking directly to your subordinates without reference to you. The decisions are not important ones but you feel you need to check the habit sooner rather than later. You believe your boss has merely been thoughtless, but he takes offence easily if he thinks he's being criticized.

Whether or not you recognize these actual examples as coming close to home, others like them will be part of your normal workload. In each instance there is a practical issue affecting the volume or quality of work which needs to be put right. But there are no standard solutions because an individual – with his unique personality, needs and motivations – is involved. The right solution for Victoria's problem would not necessarily be right for Mary, who is a different person; you cannot approach a senior manager in the same way as you would approach a junior one.

Does problem solving matter?

The answer to that question is obvious, but before passing on too quickly it may be worth while considering just how much it matters. In a small business problems show up very quickly: snags in the process or underperformance by individuals can have an immediate financial effect, and action not taken or delayed can lead to disaster. In big businesses, where there is more fat and more time, single problems have less effect on the whole of the enterprise, and managers can often get away with poor problem solving (perhaps in the hope that the problem will go away) for long periods of time. But the cumulative effects – multiplied if several managers are falling short in the same way – can eventually be even more disastrous. Many businesses which have fallen behind in the competitive race, or have disappeared altogether, can trace their difficulties back to poor problem solving at different levels of management.

If problem solving has been important in the past, it is going to be even more important in the future. The world is becoming a very tough place for the establishment and growth of businesses – as redundancies and bankruptcies so vividly show. Success will go to those who have well motivated work forces and who operate with smaller numbers of highly productive people. That means that the consequences – good or bad – of the individual's perform- ance will have a much greater effect, and that the manager's capacity to solve his problems will be a key skill. The intro- duction of sophisticated technology will in no way reduce the dependence of the business on such skills. As K.J. Lockyer, Professor of Operations Management at the University of Bradford, has written:

> First and last, however, the production manager works with people... Even in the most 'high-tech' organisation the production manager will find most of his time is spent on dealing with people problems, talking, resolving per- sonal and employment difficulties, motivating and explaining. An inarticulate production manager could not do his task at all. (*Daily Telegraph*, 13 May 1986)

Why are people so poor at problem solving?

Numerous research studies have shown that the very people you might expect to be good at solving problems are often very poor at it. Therapists, counsellors, social workers and clergymen are all professionally concerned with problem solving; we even call them the 'helping professions'. Yet studies show that their effectiveness at problem solving is, on average, low. This is strange when we recall that they have often had several years of training in these matters; and even stranger when studies appear that suggest that the more training they have had the poorer they are likely to be at problem solving. Why should this be so; and what can managers learn from it?

Problem solving is a skill, not an academic discipline

One reason is that problem solving is a skill which cannot be acquired simply by the academic study of relevant subjects such as psychology or sociology or medicine. This does not mean that a good knowledge of these subjects is not important or, for some professions, essential, but that unless the skills have also been mastered, it cannot be put to use in effective problem solving. For some personalities high academic standards can even be a block; they become a substitute for skills, or a retreat from real life – where the problems are – to the safety of the study or the library. Who would you choose as a guide – a man who has become an expert in the subject of climbing mountains from reading books, or an unlettered local who has been climbing them all his life?

> A friend of mine for many years, now dead, had an impressive theoretical knowledge. He must have read every book on psychology ever written. He knew the mysticism of East and West, regularly meditated, and could often be found in the office standing on his head in a yoga position. He was a fund of information, and I learnt a very great deal from him – perhaps more than I have from any other single person. Yet he had to be asked to resign from an important management position because his staff would not work for him. Later, when he was employed as a senior adviser at his head office, other executives would try to avoid him. They were afraid that he would treat them to an endless lecture, little of which they would understand.

Skills are often learnt best through feedback

A second reason is that human beings tend to learn skills by feedback. Thus, even an exceedingly complex skill such as driving a car can be mastered by most people because they can see the immediate effect of their actions, and they learn quickly the relationship between what they do and the outcome. But problem solving often does not seem to have a measurable outcome and so the helper has little or no way of knowing how well he is doing. The person who has asked for help may profess himself satisfied, and confident that the problem has been solved; but for all the helper knows the situation is unchanged or may revert quickly to where it was. This is even more difficult for long courses of treatment such as psychoanalysis where it has been argued that the same proportion of untreated people get better merely through the passage of time.

Are managers in a different position? There is good reason to suppose they ought to be. Their work is essentially practical, and the problems they need to tackle are often short term and have outcomes which can be seen. If they have often had little or no training at least they are not tempted to retreat into theory. Yet so many managers find problem solving difficult. They report that they often don't know where to start, they have confused conversations which lead nowhere, or they end up by giving a lecture. And the very same problem attached to the very same person comes up week after week – still unsolved. What is the answer?

The need for a systematic approach

It is becoming quite clear through experimental research that the answer lies in using a systematic method of solving problems. Several different methods have been developed, some long and some short, but they all share the same characteristics. Successful problem solving requires:

- a shared understanding by the manager and the presenter of how the problem looks from the presenter's point of view.

- an exploration to find the source of the problem and to identify what has to change.

- the establishment of practical and measurable goals adequate to bring about change.

- monitoring the achievement of the goals, and thus getting feedback.

Inertia and commonsense

Your immediate reaction may be that these principles are simply commonsense; how else would anyone think problems could be solved? And that is quite true, but there is rather more to it than that. If it is such commonsense we should be wondering why so few people employ the principles regularly. The reason may simply lie in the fact that many of us are a little bit lazy and disinclined to make the intellectual effort involved. And since life passes by for a manager so quickly, we really have no time to stop and think about it.

Another reason, perhaps more serious in its implications, is that few of us have ever received training in these aspects of management; experts in human behaviour have noticed that people almost never approach a problem systematically unless they have been trained to do so. It is significant in the light of Professor Lockyer's remarks that while a manager may often receive technical training, including professional qualifications, he is much less likely to be trained in the crucial task of managing people.

Skills take time and practice to acquire

But there may be a third reason. I have described problem solving as a *skill*, and skills are not acquired studying in an armchair. When you first learnt to ride a bicycle your parents or your friends probably explained the basic principles to you, but I doubt if that helped much when you went solo for the first time. If you persisted, through skinned knees and tears, you eventually found you had acquired the skill of basic balance and steering. You had a good deal more to learn, of course – stopping, for instance; then roadcraft, the Highway Code, and so on. The principles could only take you so far – practice was necessary to master the skill. And so it is not enough to know how to solve problems, you have to be practised in the skills. That takes persistence through the skinned knees and tears of management.

Some of the skills which are used in problem solving are

not acquired speedily. It is not that they are complex, but they are unfamiliar – we have to develop new habits and new approaches, and these are awkward until we have grown used to them. But, as I hope you will discover as you begin to master them, they not only enable you to become a good problem solver but they are useful to you in a whole range of other activities – including those which have nothing to do with your business life.

How you might use this book

Have you ever had the experience of buying a book because its title or its description seemed to answer a long felt need – and then, having decided after a quick read that it was interesting but rather hard work, slipped it into a bookshelf meaning to return to it one day? I have – come and look at my bookshelf! But you will have realized from what I have just written about the acquisition of skills that this will scarcely do. So here is a suggestion:

Every chapter has an overview at the beginning and a summary at the end. You may like to read all of these throughout the book; it will only take a few minutes. When you have done so, read through the book quite quickly, using a soft pencil to mark the margin when anything strikes you as particularly interesting. (Even if you progress no further this will impress anyone you might lend it to.)

Now pause and consider. You acquired the book because you believed that you needed to improve your problem solving ability. You have realized that the mere possession of the book will not bring about a transfer of knowledge, and that a mere reading will not make you skilled. Given that this will require study and practice over a period of time, do you still want to improve? Will the time and effort involved be repaid by your greater effectiveness as a manager? If your intention is still firm consider the Benjamin Franklin self-organizer.

The Benjamin Franklin self-organizer

Franklin wished to improve the way he lived his life in a number of respects. But he realized that, just as a gardener does not attempt to weed the whole garden at once but concentrates on one bed at a time, so he would have to concentrate on one habit at a time in order to succeed. He made a list of thirteen habits and assigned each one to a week of the quarter. He kept a little notebook by him so that he could record his successes and failures on a daily basis. But, and he emphasized this, he only worked on one habit at a time – the others were left to their ordinary chance. By the end of a quarter he had covered all his desired habits, and he was ready to go through the list again.

Applying the self-organizer to mastering problem solving

If you have read through the book you will have seen how pertinent Benjamin Franklin's method is to the achievement of goals. By choosing a concrete goal, concentrating on it, and recording results, you will give yourself the best chance of succeeding.

The book falls into five stages, corresponding to the five stages of the problem solving method. Each stage has its particular skills (although many of these can be used throughout), and each skill has to be thought about and practised. As you learn about each skill assign a period of time – from a day to a week – to practice by incorporating it into your normal management duties. Notice that the practice does not take any *time* since it does not add to your tasks, it merely improves the way you carry them out. But it does take concentration. The method I use is to make a little note in my diary, and I also attach a note to my telephone. This gives me a frequent reminder during the day. At the end of the day you should record the number of instances in which you have practised the skill against your objective; and you may like to rate your standard of achievement.

It makes sense to tackle the skills in the order they appear since this will enable you to concentrate on each of the five stages separately over a period of time. But this does not have to be so since the skills have broad applications, and you will have (or be able to make) many opportunities to practise them outside the problem solving process.

Share the book with a friend

Is there anyone else in your organization who is interested in learning how to solve problems face to face? If so, get them a copy to read, too – and work on it together. This will enable you to discuss the ideas, and strengthen your persistence since you can report to each other on progress. The book is also useful as a basic text for a small group training course.

Summary

- Most problems which a manager faces in his ordinary work come attached to people. Getting the human element right is needed for a successful solution.

- Unless managers are good at problem solving their businesses will suffer; this is increasingly important today when the performance of a few individuals can be critical for success or failure.

- Surprisingly, standards of problem solving in the 'helping professions' are not high. This seems to be because there is often little feedback for guidance, and because training is academic rather than practically based.

- Managers would seem to have an advantage here, but even they are likely to fail unless they are using a systematic method, and have mastered the skills which are needed through deliberate practice.

- The full value of this book can only be obtained through using it in an organized way. It is suggested that after an overview of the text the manager should plan to practise the skills by concentrating on them one at a time. The Benjamin Franklin method may help. Working with a colleague or a small group is excellent.

2   The LEGUP Model

The LEGUP model for problem solving is explained, and illustrated by an example. In examining whether such a model is appropriate the possibilities of it being artificial, inflexible, manipulative, or too lengthy for practical use are considered. The value of the model as a means of staff development is considered.

The stages of problem solving

In the previous chapter I listed the four steps required for effective problem solving:

- a shared understanding by the manager and the presenter of how the problem looks from the presenter's point of view.

- an exploration to find the source of the problem and to identify what has to change.

- the establishment of practical and measurable goals adequate to bring about change.

- monitoring the achievement of the goals and thus getting feedback.

To these four stages I have added a fifth because it is often necessary to make sure that the presenter has the resources to achieve the goals which he has adopted. And so we have a five-stage model, set out below. This is the basic model which will be followed throughout the book.

Listening
Exploring
Goal setting
Underpinning
Pursuing

You will have noticed that the initial letters of each stage spell 'LEGUP' – which is an appropriate mnemonic since the object of problem solving is to give the presenter a leg up towards finding a good solution. Relating these stages to the basic steps of problem solving is straightforward:

1 *Listening*: the manager is listening to the presenter in order to see the problem from the presenter's point of view.

2 *Exploring*: the manager and the presenter are exploring the problem together in order to establish its real nature, and what has to be changed in order to solve it.

3 *Goal setting*: they agree on the concrete and measurable goals which they believe will bring about the change.

4 *Underpinning*: this is the underpinning or the support the presenter may need in order to achieve the goals – for example, additional training.

5 *Pursuing*: this is the pursuit, or follow up, to discover whether the goals are being achieved and are solving the problem.

I suggested in the last chapter that poor problem solving was associated with lack of system, lack of feedback and lack of practice at the necessary skills. The model gives a systematic method of tackling problem solving, and so achieves the first condition for success. Establishing measurable goals and using Pursuit, or follow up, automatically provides feedback to help the manager and the presenter judge their progress. This fulfils the second condition for good problem solving. The skills will be dealt with fully in the course of the book, and a method for mastering them was suggested in the previous chapter.

LEGUP in action

In order to put the LEGUP model into context, here is an example – taken from real life – of the model in action.

The Listening stage

> One afternoon Beryl's manager notices that she is sitting at her desk looking glum and depressed. He invites her into his office and tells her that he believes something is wrong; would she like to talk about it?
>
> At first Beryl is monosyllabic and speaks with long pauses, but her manager listens attentively and patiently, and gradually she opens up. It turns out that she's extremely bored; occasionally there's a heavy workflow, and then she's content, but most of the time she feels she's sitting around uselessly while the clock drags its way onwards.
>
> When Beryl has had her say, her manager sums up the problem as she, Beryl, sees it and feels about it. He checks with her that he's got the right picture.

The Exploring stage

> Beryl's manager asks her what additional work she would be enthusiastic to take on. At first she says: 'Anything'; but when they get down to examples they discover that she doesn't really want to take very much responsibility or initiative – she would rather have a routine work flow which occupies her time without too much pressure on her mental processes. Her manager asks her how she would feel about moving to a department which has a higher proportion of routine work. No, Beryl wouldn't want to do that – she likes her immediate colleagues and wouldn't want to leave them. Her manager invites her to look at the fact that she wants routine work and yet prefers to stay in a department where this isn't easily available. Beryl

smiles ruefully and admits the inconsistency. Given that, says her manager, would she be prepared to try work which was a little more demanding than her present activities but would still not be too difficult? 'Yes,' says Beryl, 'provided somebody trains me.'

The Goal setting stage

After some further discussion they decide on a task which Beryl feels she could tackle, and which will occupy her one day a week. 'Let's see how you get on with that,' says her manager; 'if it goes well we'll explore some other possibilities.'

The Underpinning stage

The manager asks a senior member of the department to join them. He explains the situation and arranges for Beryl to be trained in her new function. He makes a mental note that the department's work will need some readjustments to fit in with her new role.

The Pursuing stage

He asks the senior department member to keep an eye on Beryl's progress; and he tells Beryl that he's made a note in his diary to see her in a month's time. If she's settled into her new job by then they'll talk about the next step.

How LEGUP helped

Beryl's problem was a simple one, chosen merely to illustrate the LEGUP framework in action. Nevertheless it is useful to reflect on what might have happened if stages of the framework had been left out. The manager started by listening to Beryl's story in a particular way; he was trying to see the picture – both the facts and the feelings – from *Beryl's* point of view. He then communicated to her that he had done so. Was that important? Think back to the last time you wanted to communicate something which deeply concerned you. Was it important that the person you were speaking to really understood the point you were trying to make, and how you felt about it – even if he didn't necessarily agree with you? You might have thought the rest of the conversation a waste of time if the other person hadn't understood the point you were making in the first place.

Exploring the problem was also essential. Beryl hadn't really thought through her feelings, and her manager – by getting her to look at them – helped her to see that, to some extent, the problem was caused by her own unwillingness to take on more challenging work. And that clarified the problem for both of them: it was how to find work which would interest Beryl, and yet would not be too demanding.

If the conversation had ended there nothing would have been achieved. But the manager led the conversation on towards setting a practical goal for Beryl to tackle. By itself it probably wouldn't solve the problem, but it was a first constructive step from which further progress could be made.

In this instance Beryl had made it clear that she would need help (Underpinning) to achieve the goal. This is not necessary, of course, when the presenter is able to achieve the goals without it; but it is important for the manager to check this out. A goal which the presenter is not equipped to achieve will only result in disappointment or drain self-confidence.

Pursuit, or follow up, was arranged by the manager, as a final step. It gave Beryl a motivation to see the goal through, it assured her that he would continue to care about the outcome, and it would give him the opportunity to measure progress and, perhaps, to move her on to a more ambitious goal.

Using a model

The idea of using a framework or a model for problem solving may, at first sight, seem inappropriate. We are talking about dealing with human beings, and the valued relationships we have with our colleagues. A model might be seen as inhuman and artificial – as if we could reduce people to a formula. It may also appear inflexible: the Beryl problem may have worked just as I described it but experience shows that real life is usually much more complicated. After all, the presenter doesn't know the model, and may resist being dragged through stages of our own devising. And then people tend to be complex: they wander off the point, they don't always reveal their true feelings, they don't always carry out what they've undertaken. How can a model deal with all that? Using a model can also be manipulative: it is arguably a deliberate and skilled way of ensuring that other people dance to our tune. Can it be right to engineer our relationships with other people, even our subordinates, by using techniques which give us the advantage? And, looking at the practical aspects, the model may be too lengthy for many business situations. After all, a manager often only has a minute or two to solve a problem; he will rarely have the time to work through a five-stage model which could take hours.

These are important questions to examine, because no one can use a model properly if he doesn't really believe in it. Besides, examining these questions will test whether the model has the potential to deliver what it promises.

Is a model inhuman and artificial?

If your background is in sales you will probably be used to models already. Think for instance of the model for a sales interview: AIDA – Attention, Interest, Desire, Action. Like me, you probably found this formula (or one like it) very useful when you first started selling. Without it your sales interviews lacked structure, you lost your way, and ended inconclusively. And it helped you to make sure that you had covered all the necessary ground before closing the sale. With more experience, of course, the formula became habitual – although, in my case at least, it was necessary to go back consciously to the formula from time to time, otherwise I found I was lapsing into bad habits and becoming ineffective.

Salesmen have a very wide range of personalities – perhaps wider than most professions – and therefore every salesman uses the formula in a different way which reflects his own temperament. And a good salesman learns quickly to adapt the use of the formula to different customers according to his knowledge of them. One could compare such a framework with the human skeleton: our bones all look much the same; it is the flesh which goes on them which makes us recognizable and distinct individuals. Similarly the LEGUP framework may be common to all good problem solvers, but it will be used according to the individual personalities of those involved.

We were all taught at school the simple formula of: beginning, middle and end, in order to achieve good essay structure. That did not make our essays artificial – merely comprehensible. And anyone who has done public speaking will have come across the instruction: tell them what you're going to say, say it, tell them you've said it. If you have ever listened to a speaker who has not grasped that lesson – and it happens all too often – you may agree that mastering a framework has its advantages.

Is the model inflexible?

One of the best reasons for using a model is that the problem solver has to be ready for anything. He must be able to respond appropriately to the needs of the moment, and yet not lose his way. A framework held in the back of his mind tells him where he is, and reminds him when he is off track. It is the traveller without a map and a compass who does not dare to stray; the traveller who knows how to get back on course can take excursions with impunity.

While Beryl is explaining how she feels about her job she is reminded of her sister who was made redundant some months ago; she starts to talk about this. Her manager listens for a few minutes, but when he is satisfied that Beryl's sister has nothing to contribute to the problem he says to her, politely but firmly: 'Perhaps we could talk about your sister another time, Beryl. But you were saying that sometimes you feel the day will never end; tell me more about that....'

Coping with new problems

It often happens that, quite late in the process, the presenter begins to reveal another problem not mentioned before. The manager has to decide whether this is a completely different problem, and needs to be dealt with on another occasion; or whether it is really part of the whole picture he is dealing with. If it is part of the picture he may need to go back to the Listening stage so that the new element can be properly incorporated into the discussion.

> Beryl and her manager have proceeded quite smoothly to the Goal setting stage. But while they are discussing new tasks Beryl might undertake, she starts to talk about her lack of education. This is clearly important to her. Her manager may decide that it has nothing to do with the first problem and that he must steer her back to the task in hand. But he may decide that her lack of education (or, more likely, her feelings about her lack of education) is the reason for her loss of confidence in undertaking more demanding work. If so he may need to understand and explore her feelings about this in order to see if they affect the solution to the problem. He might also judge, incidentally, that Beryl's feelings are so strong that she will not be able to look at the problem in hand until they have been understood. But he is able to go quickly back to the first stage of the model, if he feels he should, without losing his way and confusing them both.

Getting feedback on progress

The structure of the model is a useful guide to the progress the manager is making. For example, if the presenter is finding it hard to approach the Exploration stage with enough objectivity to establish the core of the problem it may be that the Listening stage has not been properly completed. The feelings in the presenter which have not been fully expressed may be blocking his ability to stand back and look at the nature of the problem. When the manager has spotted this he can lead the presenter back to the Listening stage. Similarly, if the presenter does not seem fully committed to reasonable goals for change it may be that he is not really convinced that he should change, or that the goals will really help the change to take place. This will often mean a return to the Exploration stage to ensure that its work has been done properly.

> When Beryl meets her manager again, in the Pursuit stage, he finds that she has made little progress. She has not accomplished her goal, and she is as unhappy as she was before. Her manager will have to track back through the stages in order to discover what has gone wrong. Was she given the right help to perform the goal? Did she really accept the goal as valuable and achievable? Were her assurances in the Exploration stage that she really wanted to do what was necessary to improve things just wishful thinking?

This is the feedback aspect of the model working. We so often have the frustrating experience of working hard at a problem, and then discovering later that nothing has been achieved. The model provides a useful check, helping us to identify the stage of the process which went wrong; and, of course, telling us what has to be put right.

Is the model manipulative?

Handling people is acknowledged as a desirable managerial skill, manipulating them is not. Yet the words have the same basis (*manus* is the Latin for hand). The line is difficult to draw, and depends to a large extent on the personal values of the manager. To my mind LEGUP is about as far away from manipulation as handling people can get. Behind the method lie some implicit, important assumptions.

The presenter wants to solve the problem

It assumes that people, faced by a problem, really want to solve it in a constructive way. This is not always obvious: presenters may come to us charged with negative feelings, obstinate – even sullen. They can give every impression that they are less interested in finding a solution than in making a point. They may not believe that a solution is possible. Yet, at heart, they would really like a solution – if only someone could show them how to discover it. Of course this will not always be true: occasionally an individual may be intent on destruction, with a mind closed to the possibility of change. At least the model will help you recognize this quickly. But in almost all instances this will not be so; the presenter will be looking for the help you can give, even though he may not always be conscious of it at first.

Who solves the problem?

A second assumption about the model is that problem solving is a *mutual* task. That is, the role of the manager is ideally one of helping the presenter solve his own problem. The manager provides the framework, helps the process along, can offer advice from his own experience, can often make the arrangements required for necessary underpinning – but the presenter is the leading character, and the manager only supporting cast. There are stout practical reasons for this. Unless the presenter is able to understand the problem for himself, and to commit himself willingly to a solution, it is not likely to work very well. Nor will he benefit very much from an imposed solution to which he has not contributed. But if he has solved the problem for himself he will have learnt from the experience. Good problem solving, along these lines, can be an important way of developing staff for the future.

The manager's attitudes

All this presupposes certain attitudes in the good problem solving manager. He has to have faith in the natural motivation of human beings to behave in constructive ways. If at heart he believes that people only react to sticks and carrots then there will be no space in his mind for the idea that they may want to fulfil themselves through doing a satisfactory job of which they can be proud. It is, if you think about it, the stick and carrot manager who is manipulative – alternatively tempting and forcing his subordinates to play his game; the manager who takes into account the human desire for self-fulfilment avoids manipulation because he is helping his subordinates to achieve what they already want to achieve for themselves.

Faith in subordinates' abilities

He must also have faith in his subordinates' basic competence. Managers continually come up against difficulties caused by their belief that they can always do a job better than anyone else. ('If you want a job done properly, you'd better do it yourself.') This touching belief in our own omnipotence is often a source of amusement to our staff. Even if it is true, which can hardly be so all the time, we have to act as if it were not so. It is better to have ten jobs reasonably well done – because of our guidance and training – by ten people than to have one job superbly done by ourselves. Failure to trust people to do a good job has the certain outcome that they will stop bothering; eventually they will become unable to do a good job – and so we will have proved ourselves right after all! And, of course, we shall never be promoted – who would promote someone so obviously capable of what he's doing, and who has no member of his staff fitted to succeed him? Quite a good test of when a manager has reached the highest post he is competent to hold is when he is unable to lead others to perform the necessary tasks as well as or better than he can.

Fortunately no one needs to be caught in this trap of his own delusions. While clearly everyone has their limitations (Beryl may never be able to take on jobs above a certain level) people are able to achieve surprising things if they are helped to reach out for them. Time and again I have been surprised at what an individual who had been written off as a person of limited capacity could handle when he set his mind to it. The good problem solving manager needs to be optimistic about his staff's capacities, and often his confidence in them is the trigger which enables them to have confidence in themselves. His job is to help them to reach their own potential, and he cannot do this unless he believes that the potential is there.

The model takes too long to be practical

Asking if the model is too long is like asking if someone's legs are too long: if they reach the floor, they'll do. In fact the model can take just a few minutes or several hours – the length is dictated by the problem and the participants, not by the model. For any problem, however brief, to be solved it is necessary for the problem to be communicated, for it to be understood, for the actions to put it right to be established, for the manager to be sure that the ability to take these actions exists, and for the outcome to be checked. It may take only five minutes, and some of the stages – such as Underpinning – may be implicit. But unless the stages are accomplished the problem will not be solved.

Managers have to invest time wisely, and this will sometimes mean delegating the solving of less important problems to others. But it is always bad time management to use ineffective methods – then there is no return on the investment. The problem which returns again and again because it has not been dealt with in the right way on the first occasion is the great waster of time and efficiency. Using LEGUP efficiently will enable you to save both.

The LEGUP approach as a means of staff development

The aim of any manager who hopes to achieve success through the success of his people is to have bright, intelligent staff who can perform their jobs with as little supervision as possible. Consequently he must be working to teach his staff to solve their own problems wherever they can. LEGUP is very helpful here: by taking staff regularly through the systematic stages, and explaining why he is doing so, he will be showing them a method they can use themselves. As he demonstrates the skills of the process, and these are seen to work, staff will gradually pick up and begin to employ the skills for themselves. And since the method involves the problem presenter rather than the manager in finding the solution, staff quickly learn that they are not going to be spoon-fed. They must take responsibility for their decisions and their actions. Staff grow, and so does their manager – for he is sitting on their shoulders.

Who presents the problem?

For the sake of simplicity I have, for the most part, used examples of problems which are initiated by staff. Indeed I refer to the staff member as the *presenter* of the problem, and to the person whose help is sought as the *manager*. In practice there are many instances where the manager actually initiates the process – perhaps he draws attention to poor performance, or to some difficulty a staff member may appear to be having. But the problem to be solved – and the primary responsibility for solving it – lies, nevertheless, with the staff member: the presenter.

Summary

- The model proposed for efficient problem solving is LEGUP: Listening, Exploring, Goal setting, Underpinning, Pursuing.

- LEGUP meets the criteria of being systematic and providing feedback on progress.

- The method is not artificial or inhuman because it is no more than a basic framework which will be clothed with the personality of the individual using it.

- Far from being inflexible, the model enables the manager to be much freer in handling the problem because he knows where he is. It can incorporate secondary problems which arise, and provide a check on the success of each stage.

- Because the model assumes that presenters naturally want to find solutions to problems, and because it is aimed at helping the presenter to solve problems for himself, it is the opposite of manipulative.

- The model only uses the amount of time required to solve a problem effectively. It saves the time inevitably wasted through the use of less efficient methods.

- The aim of the manager is also to help his staff to become better at solving their own problems. LEGUP works because it demonstrates a systematic method, shows useful skills in action, and encourages staff to take responsibility for their own decisions.

3   Why Listening?

Most managers know that good listening is part of their job and think, or hope, they have mastered the skill. But it is harder than it looks. Yet good listening is the foundation of good problem solving – not only does it help to clarify the problem as the presenter sees it, but it builds the trust and confidence which are required if the manager is to give real help.

Are you a good listener? That's a challenging question because every manager knows that listening is a key skill. To admit to being a poor listener is tantamount to admitting to being a poor manager. So perhaps it would be more comfortable to say that you are actually quite good at listening but realize, as with most other skills, that you could be better.

However, I am prepared to admit that, by nature, I am a poor listener. I thought I was quite good at it until I received training in real listening; then I quickly discovered how much I had to learn. I hope that by now I have become relatively skilled in the art. But I have to avoid complacency because I know, by experience, that I can easily slip back into the old bad habits.

How well do you listen?

In the last chapter I stressed that skills could not be learnt without actually carrying them out and so, to test your good intentions, I want to start with a practical exercise. Imagine yourself at work – perhaps at your desk, perhaps somewhere on the shopfloor. There's all the usual bustle and noise early on a Friday afternoon when everyone is trying to get everything out of the way ready for the weekend. You decide to have a word with Geoffrey; he joined the firm some months ago, and this may be an opportunity to get to know him better. He is rather older than most of the staff, having joined you from a previous career as a senior non-commissioned officer in the army. He is always dressed neatly, very polite, and the work you have seen from him is punctilious. After some casual conversation you gather that Geoffrey is quite glad of the opportunity to talk. He is not entirely happy with the job and wants to tell you why. Imagine that he is actually speaking to you now, and listen as carefully as possible to what he says.

'It's not that easy settling down in a civvy job – the standards are quite different of course and the sense of discipline's not the same. The work's quite straightforward, I soon got the hang of how you do things. No – and I'm sure you won't mind me speaking frankly, that's my way – it's the other people. They're not very friendly, you know. Most of them won't speak to me and, if they do, they're usually rude. Course they're not very bright, you know – most of them can scarcely read or write; and their manners – well, you wonder where they've been brought up.

Mind you, I don't suppose it's their fault. It's the way nowadays, isn't it? You can't expect anything better. You know, I used to try to help them, show them some wrinkles to save time and do a better job. But they didn't want to learn and – you wouldn't believe this – the supervisor actually told me to lay off helping them; said it wasn't my job, that I was a disruptive influence. That's the sort of thanks you get. Anyway I'm pretty browned off with the whole thing – it hasn't really worked out. Maybe I'd be better off in another job.'

Now, pause for a minute and try to recall what went through your mind while Geoffrey was speaking to you.

What did you hear?

Let's look at two quite different accounts a manager might give:

1　'As Geoffrey was talking to me my first thought was: thank goodness I don't work with him. He sounded conceited, patronizing – and I can just see what his supervisor means by calling him a disruptive influence. Wherever he goes he'll have to learn that he's not in the army any longer; after all he's starting at the bottom in a new career. I'm really quite glad the others are knocking some sense into him. If they can just get the message across, and maybe I can help with that, he may get over this patch, and settle down to being a useful person.'

2　'As Geoffrey was talking to me I realized how thoroughly fed up he was with his work situation. He's had lots of experience and done well in his previous career, and he's hurt because no one wants to take what he can offer. And then, to cap it all, even the supervisor - who really should be able to recognize his abilities – sees him as a nuisance rather than a help. He really doesn't know what to do about it, and he feels the only solution may be to leave us.'

Listening to ourselves, or listening to the speaker?

Neither of those accounts is inaccurate. But they are given from two different points of view: the first is an expression of the manager's reaction to Geoffrey, the second is an expression of how the manager sees Geoffrey's perspective on the situation.

Looking more closely at the first account, the manager is judging and analysing the situation. He has immediate sympathy with Geoffrey's colleagues and he is clear about the root causes of the problem. He then goes on to consider some actions which might put the matter right, and allow him to retain a good worker. In fact this is what we all normally do: we hear what is being said and, using our feelings and our judgement, we start to process the information – responding to it and beginning to formulate the decisions which it may call for. And that means that we are not listening – because listening means taking into our understanding what is actually being said and felt by the speaker. But it's impossible to do that at the same time as we are reacting to it and analysing it in our own terms.

The manager giving the second account has put himself into Geoffrey's shoes: he is allowing himself to see the world as Geoffrey sees it, to feel it as he feels it, to experience it as he experiences it. But for most of us 'allowing' is the wrong word. The effort to force ourselves away from our own viewpoint and to stretch our imagination around someone else's viewpoint is considerable. It doesn't seem natural. And it's made very much more difficult when – as perhaps in this case – you really do feel that the speaker has asked for all he's getting.

Another example

Just to test how difficult it really is I am going to provide another example. Listen to it again, as you did to Geoffrey, and then try to summarize – without making any judgements – what the situation looks and feels like from the speaker's viewpoint; try to put yourself inside his skin, and look out through his eyes.

'Frankly, in our business we don't have too much time to think about the customer. That's because we really only do emergency work. You see, if someone's got a burst pipe, or maybe his roof's given way and the rain's pouring in, he's not in a very strong bargaining position. I mean, you can charge him twice the going rate – three times if it's after hours – and he won't complain. Does that sound hard? Well, look at it this way: nine times out of ten the fellow's been saving money for years by neglecting his maintenance; he's just paying it all at once. Besides, the people around here aren't short of the ready – they've all got nice fat jobs in Town; and they'd be the first to squeeze you till the pips squeaked if they had the chance. I don't see why my wife and kids shouldn't have some of the good things of life like everyone else; and I'm not going to lose sleep over who pays for it, providing it's honest money.'

Now, pause for a moment and try to see the situation as the speaker sees it.

Good listening is hard, but worthwhile

If, as I imagine, you lack sympathy for the speaker in this case, you'll find it very hard to stop your own feelings and judgements from getting in the way. You may even feel that the very action of allowing yourself to see the picture from the speaker's viewpoint somehow puts you into the position of agreeing with it. Good listening is a very demanding skill: it requires great concentration, and the readiness to suspend our own natural feelings and reactions so that we can grasp the natural feelings and reactions of the speaker. Communication skills are usually seen as the ability to transmit a message completely; in fact (though this is often forgotten) they also include the ability to receive the message completely. I would need to have some very good reasons for going through this, often uncomfortable, process; and fortunately there *are* very good reasons, because listening is the first and vital stage on which the whole of good problem solving depends.

The importance of listening

Good listening is the foundation of successful problem solving because:

- It builds the relationship between presenter and manager which is necessary for the mutual task of problem solving.

- It allows the presenter's feelings – which are part of the reality of the situation – to be recognized and given full weight.

- It helps to ensure that the real concerns of the presenter are expressed, not just the superficial ones.

- It helps the presenter to start sorting out the confusions in his own mind through the process of articulating them.

- It provides the emotional conditions which help the presenter to be open to the changes which may be required to solve the problem.

Building the right relationship

I shall have to leave the explanation of the inner nature of relationship to the psychologist, the philosopher or the theologian – without any great hope that they will be able to help very much. But I do know what a good relationship *feels* like, and that it is a necessary background for mutual and constructive work. Relationships exist at a variety of levels, some of which are inappropriate for the business environment. For problem solving there have to be trust, concern, and shared understanding of the elements involved. Liking each other undoubtedly helps, but I doubt if it is essential. I would rather use the word 'love', while recognizing that it is unfamiliar in this context. I mean no more than that to want to help a person to overcome a difficulty, to fulfil themselves, to be happier – and to do so for their sake rather than for one's own – is a form of loving.

Good listening is a powerful means of building a relationship. This relates to the common experience that the more we communicate with people and understand their way of life, their values and their interests the closer we feel to them. And this applies not only to individuals but also to groups – even countries and power blocs. But good listening, in the way I have described it, works at an even deeper level. In so far as it succeeds in enabling the listener to put himself, so to speak, right inside the other person and to see the world as he sees it, a relationship bond is formed from the shared understanding. I have suggested that listening in this way can sometimes lead us towards beginning to agree with someone whose opinions and approach we naturally dislike. This clearly has its dangers,

but it has its advantages, too: just occasionally we might
discover that there is more to be said for the opposing view
than we have ever suspected.

> Joe produces regular reports. They are fairly routine and do not
> change much from month to month. Usually you give them a
> quick glance, and then file them for future reference. On one
> occasion, however, you read a report through in detail: it seems
> to you to be poor work – careless, and omitting some important
> information. When challenged with this Joe says that he finds
> writing the reports extremely frustrating. When he started he
> was conscientious, but when he realized that no one read or
> commented on his work he felt very discouraged, and could
> see no point in giving his best when the only recipient was a
> filing cabinet. While one part of you felt that Joe should have
> done the job he was paid for irrespective of the outcome,
> another part recognized that Joe had a point – indeed you might
> well have reacted in the same way if you had been in Joe's
> shoes.

Good managers know that a sincere concern for their people
is important. But in the rackety crowded life of business it is
hard to maintain this continuously; there is not always
enough time to care. But staff are very sensitive, and the
simulation of care which is often the easiest substitute for
real concern is quickly spotted, and despised for hypocrisy.
Managers are judged, and rightly so, not by what they say
but by what they do. Good listening is a demonstration of
real care (it cannot be simulated); the speaker feels that his
problem is recognized and respected – and that means that
he, too, is recognized and respected. This leads immediately
to reciprocal feelings; and it builds confidence – confidence
in the problem presenter that he may have the capacity to
cope, and confidence that the manager will be of real assistance in solving the problem.

In this way good listening draws the participants into a
relationship of shared understanding and mutual respect.
The presenter warms to the genuine concern of the manager, and develops a sense of trust in his willingness and
ability to help. The importance of this for problem solving

can be seen by trying to imagine just how successful problem solving would be if any of these qualities were missing.

Listening for the feelings

In listening to Geoffrey and his problems about fitting in, we heard two different kinds of information. One dealt with the facts of the situation – for instance, that he had tried to instruct his colleagues, or that his supervisor had criticized him for interfering. The other dealt with the feelings – Geoffrey's desire to help, his disdainful attitude towards the upbringing of younger people, his hurt pride at the supervisor's reaction. Managers are used to dealing with facts: they are solid, hard edged, capable of being checked. Feelings are more difficult: it's hard to pin them down, you can't refute them by quoting contradictory feelings, they are subjective by definition. And, particularly if they are strong, they bring about a reaction in the listener – we respond emotionally to the aggression of an angry speaker or to the conceit of a Geoffrey. Yet feelings are also facts: that is, it is a fact that Geoffrey feels hurt pride, that he feels so unhappy in the job that he considers leaving it. You may or may not agree that the feelings are appropriate – but Geoffrey has them, and that is part of the reality of the situation which you are hoping to resolve.

What is more, feelings can take precedence over evidence. In theory a fact is an objective incident, and reported as such; in practice facts are easily distorted in the lens of feelings – and the memory of them is highly subjective. This has often been illustrated by experiments in which witnesses are questioned about an incident they have been asked to watch, or in which interviewers have been asked to report on information given to them in an interview. It is quite unnerving to realize how inaccurate we can all be. It was unnerving for Miranda, too, when she realized she could manufacture a fact in her own mind, when she really wanted it to be true:

Miranda is in trouble with her managing director. He needed some important staff lists for a meeting with the board, and

Miranda has failed to supply them. She is upset and defensive about what has happened but, although she acknowledges her responsibility, she feels it isn't her fault. She had given her secretary explicit instructions to prepare the lists, and if the stupid girl had spent more time thinking about her work and less about romantic novels she'd have had them ready on time. After a stormy meeting with her boss she goes back to her office and really lets fly at her secretary. After the tears her secretary produces their diary and demonstrates that she was on a week's holiday at the time when Miranda was supposed to have been giving her the instruction. Miranda is now really confused: she actually has a memory of telling her secretary and yet the diary proves that she couldn't have done so.

De-fusing feelings

One of the objectives of good listening is to understand the speaker's feelings thoroughly so that they may be dealt with as an important factor in the situation. And that means suspending our own feelings for the time being to prevent them interfering with our reception or tempting us to dismiss a feeling because we don't share it. It is equally important that the very process of articulating feelings, and having them properly heard, can actually take the sting out of them. Unconstructive feelings are like mushrooms: they flourish in the dark and they need bringing out into the sunlight. It is common to bottle up all sorts of bad thoughts so that they incubate and grow; but once they have been fully expressed and listened to some of the power has been removed from them. Moreover, once they are out in the open, it is possible to look at them and judge whether they are truly appropriate.

The inability of managers to deal adequately with the feelings of the people involved in a problem, to allow them to be expressed, to accept them as valid, and to be able to help the problem presenter to come to terms with them, is one of the biggest obstacles to good problem solving. Listening from the perspective of the presenter, and suspending our reactions while doing so, is an essential technique to master.

Uncovering the real concerns

Mary went to her boss and asked him for a loan from the firm to help her with some sudden expenses. Since she was a good and reliable employee he agreed to give it to her without quibble. Indeed, he felt rather virtuous for doing so. So he was surprised, and a little hurt, when Mary didn't react with the pleasure and gratitude he expected.

What went wrong? In fact Mary's real problem was that she had landed herself in difficulties through over-enthusiastic use of plastic money. She was too nervous to say this outright, but she hoped that her boss would guess there was something more serious behind her request, or somehow – she didn't know how – make it easy for her to explain. Unfortunately her boss was already working out how to solve Mary's request while she was making it. Because he didn't listen fully he missed the messages of concern in Mary's voice; because he did not give her confidence through his full attention she felt too shy to take the matter further; by dealing with the problem so quickly he did not give her the space or the time to bring out what she really wanted to say. I hope he had the sense to react to Mary's disappointment, before she left the room, so that he could call her back and ask her if there was something else bothering her – and then to communicate that he was genuinely interested in what she had to say.

No doubt Mary could be faulted for asking her boss to play guessing games. But it so often happens in just this way – a person wants to test out the water with a relatively minor difficulty and, if all goes well, to move on to what is really the heart of the matter. Of course it is not always an embarrassing problem – as we may suppose Mary's to have been; sometimes it just seems better to approach one's boss from the flank:

Ferguson is feeling unsettled. He believes he's overdue for promotion and wonders what Mrs Grant, his MD, has in mind – if anything. He is reluctant to put the question outright, so he talks to her of his concern about the slow career development of his second in command. In this way he thinks that the MD is almost bound to raise the subject of his own next move. Once asked he will feel free to express his views. Mrs Grant, who wasn't born yesterday, picks up the vibrations but thinks the initiative should be left with Ferguson. However, her very real interest in the problem of the senior subordinate, which conveys her implicit approval of Ferguson for having raised the subject, gives him the confidence to speak directly to her about his own future.

Unless the problem presenter is given every help to bring out his real concerns then it is likely that the subsequent stages of LEGUP will be frustrated. Mary may go off clutching her loan, but still as worried as ever about her financial difficulties. Ferguson will not pursue the task of developing his subordinate if his real focus is on how to develop himself. Time will be wasted, and serious problems be unsolved, if the manager is not a skilled listener and fails to communicate his genuine openness to what the speaker really has to say.

Sorting out the confusion

People who present problems to their manager often do so in a confused way. This is not surprising because human affairs and feelings often are confused; it takes a very orderly person to think through the difficulty, sort it logically, and present a coherent picture. In fact a central task in the Exploration stage is to take the jumble that has been put forward and sort it out so that the nature of the problem, and the key elements contributing to it, may be seen. But when the Listening stage begins it may sound more like this:

'You see, it's not that Fred's a bad supervisor – I mean our section's usually ahead of objective. It's just that he's always finding fault. I can have done a first class job, and he says nothing about that – but one little mistake and he's down like a ton of bricks. Of course I'm not really a mate of his – he likes his football, and anyone who's not interested in sport gets a hard

time from him. I don't mean that I never make mistakes, after all
I'm human. And it makes me feel bad; you know, I sometimes
wake up in the middle of the night – and I'm sweating because
I've dreamt I've made a mistake, and Fred's getting at me again.
You see, there's lots of detail in my job, you need a lot of
concentration. And that's not helped when you're not sleeping.
Mind you, the others complain too – not all of them, he's got his
blue-eyed boys....'

It's possible, of course, to examine that account on the
printed page and begin to tease out the elements; although
one would need to know more before deciding on which the
key ones were. But if the speaker is encouraged through good
listening he may begin to sort the matter out for himself.
When he first starts presenting the problem what he
reproduces are the confusions in his own mind. And this may
be the first time he has ever articulated them (or articulated
them to someone ready to listen rather than to suggest
solutions before he has finished). The very process of putting
his confused thoughts into words allows him to review them
and, in doing so, to begin to sort them out. We might imagine
the dialogue continuing:

> **Manager:** So you're really unhappy because Fred's getting at
> you for small mistakes, and that's getting you so upset you don't
> sleep.

> **Presenter:** That's about it. Of course I can't blame Fred for the
> sleeping, that's down to me, I suppose. It's just the nit-picking. No,
> I suppose that's not really true – he's right to pick up mistakes,
> that's what he's paid for. It's just that he doesn't appreciate all the
> good work I do. If he did that I wouldn't care so much about the
> rest.

> **Manager:** So you think the real problem isn't his criticism, it's that
> you don't feel he appreciates that you mostly do good work.

> **Presenter:** Yes, I'm getting all the kicks and none of the rewards.

If you study the manager's contribution to that dialogue you
will see that he has done no more than to reflect back to the

presenter what he has said, thus demonstrating that he has
been listening carefully. In the next chapter I shall have
some important things to say about the listener's responses,
but for the moment the point I am trying to demonstrate is
that the presenter, simply by looking at what he has himself
said, is enabled to start disentangling it. He has begun to see
that Fred's attitude towards football, and the lack of sleep,
are not central to the problem. It's not even the fault-
finding, but the lack of appreciation which is really bothering
him.

Since problem solving is a mutual process in which,
ideally, the presenter should be doing most of the work, the
more he can sort out for himself with the stimulus provided
by a good listener the better. It often happens that a problem can resolve itself completely through this process: the
presenter sees for himself what is wrong and then decides
what steps he must take to put matters right. But, even if the
problem remains, progress will have been made through the
part good listening can play in making it possible for the
presenter to begin disentangling the confusion.

Listening gives the manager the right to help

It is true that, in a legal sense, a manager has the right to do
what may be required to solve a problem in the area he
controls; but the psychological right follows different rules.
If the problem presenter is being expected to face up to the
problem, to explore his weaknesses and his strengths which
may have contributed, to accept his responsibilities without
defensiveness, an atmosphere of trust and a recognition of
his manager's concern will be necessary. And good listening
is the foundation for these. The third factor I mentioned was
a shared understanding of the elements involved. When this
is lacking a manager disqualifies himself as a helper:

> 'I had a chat with Holroyd this morning. I wanted to tell him that I
> was fed up with Fred, and get the whole thing sorted out.
> Useless, of course. I tried to explain about all the nit-picking but
> Holroyd just said that if I made mistakes then he expected Fred

to pick them up. Then he said I was much too sensitive, and maybe I should get some pills to help my sleeping. He just didn't understand what I was driving at.'

Perhaps you have had the experience of going to a doctor for some complaint which worries you, and being in and out of the surgery in three minutes. The doctor asks you some cursory questions, tells you there's nothing wrong, and sends you on your way, past the long queue of patients waiting outside. You may also have had the experience of a doctor who takes your worry seriously, listens to you carefully, asks questions, and gives you an examination. He then tells you that there appears to be nothing seriously wrong but suggests you come back if the systems persist. In terms of medical treatment both doctors have behaved identically. But which of the two sends you away with your worry at least a little diminished? Which of the two would you prefer to come back to if your symptoms continue? Which of the two gives you greater confidence in his medical skill?

Good listening means that, as far as possible, the manager understands the problem from the presenter's point of view. When the presenter recognizes this he knows that the help he will receive is based on a solid foundation of shared understanding. At the psychological level the manager has earned the right to move on into the Exploration stage.

Summary

- Most people do not truly listen. They may hear what is being said but they are distracted by their instinctive response which is to analyse the information while it is being given, and to react to it with their own feelings.

- The essential characteristic of good listening is the ability to understand what is being said – facts and feelings – from the speaker's viewpoint, rather than the listener's.

- Because good listening is so hard a manager will need adequate reasons to master and use the skill. In fact, such listening is essential to effective problem solving.

- Good listening builds the relationship needed for co-operation in problem solving; it allows the presenter's feelings – an important factor – to be aired and taken into account; it helps the presenter to express his real concerns – which may not be revealed immediately; it gives the presenter opportunity and encouragement to begin to see the problem more clearly for himself; it gives the presenter confidence in the manager since he knows that the problem has been recognized and understood.

4 Listening Skills

Full listening requires a quite different approach from conversational listening. A number of skills have to be mastered: in particular, the ability to give mirror summaries which communicate that the listener has really understood, and which give the speaker the chance to review what he has been saying. The feelings as well as the words need to be heard and reflected; mastering non-verbal communication can be important for this.

I have stressed that the fundamental difference between the listening we do habitually and the true listening necessary for problem solving lies in the readiness and ability to hear the picture from the viewpoint of the speaker rather than that of the listener. I asked a very experienced listener to describe to me what it felt like. This was how she put it:

'I find myself sitting back, very relaxed – even my pulse rate drops. I have to change from being an equal participant in a conversation into someone who is receiving information. It takes enormous concentration because I have to dismiss from my mind all the thoughts prompted by what the other person is saying, and just hear it as it comes. It's not only the words, of course, it's the 'music' behind the words – the tone of voice tells me a lot about the feelings. And I listen with my eyes: you can 'hear' a great deal just by watching how a person sits or the expression on their face.

Of course I notice points which I think may be important –

maybe there is an inconsistency which I spot, or a remark which seems very significant – but I check myself from thinking about it; it sort of pings in my mind like a cash register and I store it for later use. In fact I say very little – mostly encouraging noises from time to time. I'll ask for clarification if I simply don't understand what's been said; but I try not to let that hold up the flow. And, at what seems the right point, I try to summarize what I've understood.

It's very hard – listening. The most difficult part, I find, is not letting myself interfere mentally or emotionally with the message I'm getting.'

That account mentions most of the essential points about listening techniques, and these are worth examining in rather more detail.

The mind of the listener

In the previous chapter I dealt with this question, but the account above makes the point that a quite deliberate switch is needed from our normal conversational listening. Conversational listening is two-way: while the other person is talking we are probably already framing our next contribution, and we feel entitled to an equal share of the speaking time – since we are equal participants. Full listening is one-way: the speaker holds the stage and the listener is the recipient – he says very little (although, as I shall describe later, what he does say is crucial). And this is marked by a change in the physical attitude of the listener. Some listeners sit back, others come forward with their bodies as they bring their full attention to bear; but they are always relaxed and quiet. It is necessary to communicate to the speaker that they have the full concentration of the listener; that they have the time and the space to say what they need to say.

This is easy to practise. Imagine that you are sitting in the chair you are using now, and that someone sitting opposite you is telling you something really fascinating, something which truly interests you. What the speaker is saying is quite complicated to follow, and you want to catch every word.

Now get into the position you would naturally take up in those circumstances... .

Notice what has happened to your body. When I try this I find that I come forward a little in my seat, but my body is relaxed – not rigid. My hands are loosely clasped in front of me, my legs are uncrossed. My head is stretched a little towards the imaginary speaker and my eyes, although still, are watching him directly. The position you took up may have been different in detail, but you would have been recognized by the speaker as someone who was really interested in what they had to say.

For the second part of the exercise imagine that the office bore has come in to see you with one of his endless detailed complaints he insists on telling you about. You have a crowded day and you're anxious to fit in a quick snack lunch before your first meeting this afternoon. Now get into the position you would naturally take up in those circumstances... .

Notice what has happened to your body. I find that I seem to close up; my legs cross and I turn the angle of my body away from the speaker. I become more tense and I tend to compress my lips. While I try to watch the speaker I find that my eyes wander, often – I fear – towards my wristwatch. When I analyse the differences in my physical reactions to the speakers I realize that I am communicating two very different messages – usually without being conscious at the time that I am doing so.

The silent response

In the account I quoted above the listener's responses were described as 'encouraging noises' and summarizing. The problem of describing encouraging noises in print defeats me; but I think we all have our own little grunts and half phrases which indicate that we would like the speaker to continue. Before talking about summarizing, I would like to say something about silences.

Some years ago one of my daughters, then aged ten, was given to suddenly breaking out into nonsense talk or even

singing at the family table. When I asked her why, she said
that there was a silence waiting to be filled, so she con-
siderately filled it. I know exactly what she meant. When
there is a silence in conversation many people feel awkward,
and the longer the silence the more embarrassing it becomes.
Moreover, in a work context it just seems wrong for two
people to face each other, neither speaking, and nothing
happening. But, when people are trying to explain something
they find difficult to say, or hard to articulate, silences can be
very important. A great deal can be happening under the
surface – as they collect their thoughts, or reflect on what they
have already said, or summon the courage to go on. And I
have often had the experience of accepting a long silence –
perhaps a number of minutes – only to be rewarded by the
problem presenter at last coming out with what he really
wanted to say.

So silence can actually be a positive contribution to the
process – provided that the listener, through his relaxed
posture and his continued interest, communicates that silence
is fine by him if it is helping the presenter to express himself.
Rush in, like my daughter, to fill the silence and you will
break the flow and deny the speaker the space he needs to tell
his story. If you are not accustomed to letting silences 'happen', you will find your first attempts feel uncomfortable; and
the pressure to speak will be strong. But practice helps here;
and the thought that the speaker is often combating even
greater pressure will give you courage.

However, summarizing is the main and most valuable
response of the listener. It has two functions: first, it communicates to the presenter that you have really heard and
understood him; second, it allows the presenter to see a
reflection of what he has said in your summary, and thus to
look at it through fresh eyes.

Communicating your listening

It is not sufficient that you should have heard and understood
what the presenter is trying to say, he has to *know* that you
have heard and understood. You want to start the problem

solving process from a shared understanding – and you both have to know that it has been shared. Moreover, however carefully you have tried to listen, you will still need to check that you have picked up the right message, or the message the speaker – however ineptly – was trying to communicate.

If you turn back for a moment to the example on p. 37 where the manager is responding to a complaint about a supervisor, you will notice that the responses were put in terms of the speaker's point of view. The manager did not add to what had been said; he did not try to interpret it; he did not indicate agreement or disagreement – he merely summarized as well as he could what he had understood from the speaker. Read the following example of a statement followed by the listener's summary, and see whether you think it to be a good response:

> **Foreman:** Yes, I accept that last week's batch was faulty. I've read the customer's letter and I've seen our inspector's report. I'm sick as a parrot about it, but it's simply not my fault. I can't tell you the number of times I've told the factory manager that the machine tools aren't up to the job. They just won't work to the tolerances needed. It's only because the firm's too darned mean to put in this new German equipment that we have these problems. So it's no good taking it out on me.

> **Manager:** So it's the equipment, is it? You don't think, even though you're the foreman, that you've got any responsibility for the work that goes out from your section, because the factory manager doesn't agree about the machinery.

It's a very natural response but not a helpful one – especially at the Listening stage. The manager has not heard what the foreman has been saying; what he has 'heard' is the foreman trying to shuffle responsibility elsewhere. He does not accuse him directly but, through a small but significant distortion of his response, he does so implicitly. Here is an example of another response for you to judge:

> **Manager:** Yes, I can see your problem. But the fact of the matter is that new equipment just wouldn't be financially

possible for us this year – and, believe you me, the factory
manager is arguing for it just as strongly as you. In the meantime
we have to rely on good quality control; and that simply means
we'll have to scrap poor batches from time to time.

Clearly the manager has heard part of what has been said
and has grasped some important aspects of the problem
sympathetically. But he has also missed elements which
could turn out to be important in the resolution of the
problem. Here is a third response:

Manager: So you're just as concerned about this as the rest of
us. But, as you see it, the problem lies with the machinery; and,
as long as the company doesn't put that right, it's going to
continue. You also sound a bit fed up at being blamed for
something you don't see as your fault. Have I got the picture?

You may agree that, at last, the manager has demonstrated
that he was truly listening. He has expressed his response in
the foreman's terms; he has picked up the essential facts;
and he has also picked up the feelings – the 'music' behind
the words. We don't know what the foreman will say next:
he may want to revise his statement now that it has been
reflected back to him, or confirm it; he may want to add
some more information which will be helpful. Nor do we
know at this stage whether the manager agrees with the
speaker. But giving a good listening response means that
both the problem presenter and the manager start from a
point of shared understanding of the problem as the
presenter sees it; and a strong foundation for a solution is
beginning to be laid.

The mirror summary

This last example demonstrated the use of the summary as a
means of communicating that the manager had been truly
listening; but it also operated as a mirror which enabled the
presenter to review what he had tried to communicate. And
just as a real mirror enables us to straighten a tie or adjust a

hemline, he had the opportunity to adjust his communication if the reflection was not to his liking. You may have noticed that the summary was expressed in a tentative form ('You also sound a bit fed up ... Have I got the picture?') which actually invites the possibility of revision. This tentativeness is also an important factor in indicating the exploratory nature of the dialogue right from the beginning; and it also enables the speaker to correct any misunderstanding which the listener may have made:

> **Foreman:** No, I'm not fed up with being blamed. It's just irritating because as long as people put the blame on me they're not looking at the real problem; so it won't get better.

Without this correction time might have been wasted dealing with the foreman's supposed ruffled feelings and not with the practical aspects which are, the manager knows now, the foreman's real concern.

Good summarizing responses will often trigger more material. Only the simplest problems can be expressed in a statement or two; and, realizing that his first point has been properly understood, the speaker can then continue with further points which seem to him to have a bearing on the problem. Sometimes, as I suggested in the last chapter, it is through this later material that the real problem emerges. It can also encourage the discursive speaker to go wildly off the point but, as the example of Beryl showed (Chapter 2), it is possible for the manager to steer the speaker gently back on course. Indeed, good summarizing will usually help to give a structure to the material, discouraging repetition and enabling the speaker to build up the picture he wishes to communicate, in the shortest possible time.

Practising summaries

Here are three statements which might have been made to you during the Listening stage. Take each one separately, and consider the summary you might make. Remember to express it in the terms of the speaker, reflecting back the

message you have heard. Your summary should be tentative –
as if checking that you have the right picture, and making it
easy for the speaker to revise what has been said, or to
continue.

1   'Frankly, the typing pool's a mess. You can send a tape down
    first thing in the morning, and there's no guarantee you'll get it
    back in time for the last post. Any mistakes – and you've had
    it. One way or another you can't be sure of getting any letter
    out within two days. Of course I know I'm not senior enough to
    rate a secretary but, honestly, that's false economy. Heaven
    knows what it costs the company in delays. Don't you think an
    exception could be made in my case?'

2   'No, it's the packaging that's wrong. It doesn't stand out on the
    shelf you see. Sometimes I've gone into a customer's shop and
    it's taken me quite a time to spot our stuff; no wonder it doesn't
    move. We're in a pretty competitive business, and it's really
    hard when you've put everything into getting an order and,
    the next time you call, the customer tells you he's not
    interested in repeat orders when he can't sell the first lot. It's
    not going to do my bonus any good either.'

3   'I'm really concerned. That's the second time I've been
    passed over for promotion. It's not as if I haven't got the
    qualifications. And certainly not because I've not got the
    experience. Actually I think that's maybe where the trouble
    lies: I've been around too long. Everyone thinks: poor old
    Nick, he's a fixture – can't afford to leave now with all those
    pension rights built up. Better promote the younger people in
    case they leave; and anyhow we can get them cheaper.
    Meanwhile I soldier on. But it's very shortsighted; one day
    people will realize that this firm doesn't reward loyalty –
    there's always the scrap heap for us.'

How often to summarise

For the sake of brevity I have used short examples to illustrate
the principles of summarizing; and this may have given the

impression that the listener should make a response every few sentences. In fact the frequency of summarizing will depend on the material being given, and it will usually be quite sufficient to summarize at natural breaks when a block of information has been given – and particularly when the manager feels he may lose track unless he registers the information by summarizing it. Where the problem being expressed is simple and short only one summary – at the end – may be needed. However, when the material is more complex occasional summaries will help to keep the account businesslike, and to the point; it may also help the presenter to avoid repetition through showing him clearly that he has communicated his point.

The final summary

The key summary always comes at the end. This will take into account any earlier summaries and thus try to express the whole picture as it has been understood. The agreement of the presenter to the final summary (which may be expressed in words like 'Yes, that's just about it', or simply through facial expression) is the signing off of the Listening stage – and ushers in the Exploration stage. Here is an example of a final summary:

> 'OK, Andy – I think I've got the picture; but let's just check it out. You really don't want to move to our Southern Division head-quarters. You appreciate that it means a good promotion but you think the move would be unfair on your family. Then there's the question of housing – you've looked at the prices and you're sure that, even with the company's removal package, you'll be worse off. And then you mentioned the prototype development project you've set your heart on finishing up here; you'd feel very frustrated if you had to leave it at this stage. But behind all this there's a worry that if you don't take up the offer the company will write you off, and you won't be offered promotion again. Have I got all that right?'

It looks simple on paper but good mirror summaries require skill. And it's a skill which only comes with plenty of practice.

The music behind the words

At the beginning of this chapter I quoted the experienced listener saying: 'It's not only the words, of course, it's the "music" behind the words – the tone of voice tells me a lot about the feelings. And I listen with my eyes: you can "hear" a great deal just by watching how a person sits or the expression on their face.' In fact we habitually pick up other people's feelings through their non-verbal communication without necessarily being conscious of doing so at the time. The difference is that the experienced listener has sharpened his skills so that he has become very sensitive to these messages, and therefore more accurate in identifying feelings correctly.

The methods of non-verbal communication are various. The choice of clothes, care over grooming, stance, gestures, the use of the mouth and eyes, the angle of the head, the tone of voice are just some of the ways feelings are signalled. It is, in fact, the earliest form of communication human beings use; we are born with a range of non-verbal signals programmed into us – as any one with experience of babies can confirm. For the first several months of life we use nothing else – although we quickly learn to extend our 'vocabulary' to a quite sophisticated degree. Once we have learnt to speak we can easily forget that our words are always accompanied by a sort of non-verbal commentary which is all the more revealing because we are usually unconscious of it.

Several good books have been written on the subject (see Bibliography), and therefore I will not deal with the subject further here. However, more important than reading the theory is getting the practice; that is, making oneself habitually aware of non-verbal communication through continuous observation.

Mrs Gandle asked informally for a meeting with her design manager. He was naturally a nervous man and in this case he had some reason for it. The day before he had had an overindulgent lunchtime and he had behaved rather stupidly in the office. Mrs Gandle regarded this as a momentary lapse, and wanted to do no more than throw up a warning signal. When he came into her office he had a large piece of artwork under his arm. When he sat down he propped this on his knees – like a shield to protect himself against her anger. Mrs Gandle talked to him for a few minutes about neutral office matters until she recognized that he had relaxed when he put the artwork down beside his chair. She was then able to introduce the subject of his behaviour in a low key way; and he was able to respond in a constructive rather than a defensive manner.

In this example the non-verbal evidence of the design manager's feelings was rather obvious, but we are not always lucky enough to get such a straightforward indication. But Mrs Gandle was also using her previous experience of the design director; in a business situation, it is often the differences from an individual's normal behaviour which prove to be most helpful in detecting feelings.

Here is a simple exercise. The next time you have a chance to observe someone carefully – perhaps in a train or a bus – try and decide what sort of person they are. Are they nervous or confident? Are they tidy or disorganized? Are they sporty or intellectual? Are they having a good or a bad day? If they are sitting with someone, what is their relationship to that person? – and so on. Although you may never know the answer to your analysis it should not just be a series of guesses; in each case you should be able to pinpoint the evidence which leads you to your conclusion. That exercise will perhaps do no more than make you aware of how much people tell you about themselves without saying a word. Follow it up by writing in your diary every day for perhaps a month ahead the message: *5 minutes NVC* (non-verbal communication). That will remind you to practise observation quite deliberately for five minutes every day. You might choose to observe a colleague, or a friend you meet under social circumstances – the more varied the occasions the better. Like practising tennis strokes the exercises will gradually increase your skills so that they are available to you when you need them for your work.

When does good listening stop?

Because full listening has been introduced as the principal skill of the Listening stage, it may seem that once this stage is over and Exploration can begin good listening can be abandoned. But in fact good listening is used throughout the problem solving process. Whenever the presenter is giving new information, or just trying to organize his thoughts out loud, full listening – with mirror summary responses – is the appropriate reaction. Once the message has been properly heard it is mutually shared, and can then be mutually considered.

I suggested at the end of the first chapter that some of the skills discussed in this book would have uses outside the problem solving situation. This is particularly true of listening. For, instance two people who disagree have a very much better chance of resolving their difficulty if they are ready to see the situation from the other's viewpoint through good listening. It is a powerful cement in relationships – whether business or personal. It can have a deep and lasting effect on the way one habitually sees and judges other people. But all these effects can be readily tested. And they should be. It is a skill which needs a great deal of practice; it is never fully mastered; and it easily slips away through disuse. Perhaps this is because it is an essentially selfless skill: it requires us to be more interested in the other person than we are in ourselves.

You may like to get your first practice in immediately; you don't have to wait for a problem to solve but just until you meet someone who opens up a serious conversation with you. It will be even better if it is a person who knows you well and is, perhaps, unaccustomed to having you listen to them carefully. Try using some of the skills outlined in this chapter. Even though you will probably make mistakes, or even be a little awkward through unfamiliarity, you may be pleasantly surprised by the reaction. And you may find that they talk for longer than you expect, or would ordinarily welcome. But that simply arises because they have been wanting someone really to listen to them for years. They will soon get used to your new approach – and even begin to imitate it. You will probably find out more about them in thirty minutes of good listening than you could in thirty years of ordinary relationship.

But, in the strict context of this book, the purpose of this practice is to enable you to increase your listening skills so that you can grasp the problem as the presenter sees it. Armed with this shared knowledge and understanding you can proceed to the Exploration stage.

Summary

- Unlike conversation, where the listener is an equal participant, the Listening stage requires the manager to be a receiver of information; this needs a radical change of attitude. This attitude is first signalled by the physical stance of the listener.

- The listener must accept silence comfortably so that the speaker is free to express himself without pressure.

- The listener should communicate that he has understood the message, words and feelings, by the summarizing responses he makes.

- These mirror summaries enable the speaker to focus on the reflection of what he has said; and to revise or extend it.

- Good summaries express the picture in the speaker's terms, and should be made tentatively to allow for the speaker's confirmation.

- Summaries should be used at natural points during the Listening stage; the final summary is important because the speaker's confirmation enables the Exploration stage to start.

- Non-verbal communication is an important part of listening; the skills should be developed.

- Good listening applies throughout the problem solving process. But it must be practised regularly if the skill is to be maintained and developed.

5   Why Exploration?

Exploration follows listening. It tries to make sense out of the feelings and the facts which have been presented. The objective is to identify the core problem, or problems, which need to be put right; and to do so in such a way that possible goals for change begin to present themselves. This chapter looks at the purpose of the Exploration stage, and the principles involved. The next chapter explains the practical techniques.

It is not always easy to establish the point at which the Listening stage finishes and the Exploration stage should begin. Sometimes, as I suggested in the last chapter, the manager is able to make a final summary of what he has understood, and – following the assent of the problem presenter – he is able to move smoothly into the process of exploration. But real life has a habit of being untidy, so you should not be surprised if you make one or two false starts at the time of changeover. Aim to observe the principle that the Listening stage is finished when the presenter has expressed the problem as completely as he can at that point. When he starts to bring in irrelevancies, or to repeat himself, you are being warned that it is probably time to start exploring what you have heard. But bear in mind that the process of exploration itself may bring to the presenter's mind new and relevant facts; don't be afraid to move back into the Listening stage for a time in order to pick up these dropped stitches.

The opposite difficulty may occur when the presenter has

in fact completed his own Exploration stage because the
process of expressing the problem, and hearing it reflected
through good summary, has now enabled him to understand
it. You may remember the example of the worker whose
supervisor, Fred, was always finding fault with him (p. 37).
In that instance the manager, by simply reflecting back what
he had heard, enabled the presenter to sort out the confusion, and to begin to grasp the essence of the problem.
Sometimes, in fact, the manager never has the opportunity
of saying a word: the very process of articulation may on its
own enable the presenter to clarify his mind and gain the
insights he needs.

> Karen, a new business clerk in an insurance company, had
> come to complain about her supervisor, whom she saw as
> irritable, finicky, and critical of her work. In talking about it she
> mentioned that it was: 'Just like being at home with Mum getting
> at me all the time.' She then began to see for herself why she
> reacted so badly to a superior who, after all, was not a bad sort
> really. 'Just like my Mum,' in fact.

In such instances the manager must decide whether the
Exploration stage has in fact been completed, in parallel
with the Listening stage – so that the setting of goals can
begin. But it is usually wise to check (as you will see later)
that the presenter's first understanding of the problem is
really correct.

Unravelling the tangle

Usually matters are not resolved so easily. Feelings and
incidents come out in the wrong order, confused and
jumbled. And the problem is lost in the tangle. As with a
ball of wool left in the care of the cat, there are many tag
ends which lead nowhere – and, perhaps, only one which
leads to unravelling. The purpose of the Exploration stage is
to find that right tag end; and to begin to identify the core
problem. The manager will be looking for patterns, for
common factors, for contradictions; he will challenge, and

ask the presenter to look from different points of view. He
wants to make sense of the jumble in order to find out what
has really gone wrong, and what has to change in order to
put it right.

> Charlie is clearly a talented person with a good creative mind.
> But his story is one of mediocrity; he has never got very far with
> his career, he has never written that book he's sure is in him, he
> has been divorced twice. Are all these quite separate problems
> which need to be tackled one by one? Or is there just one root
> problem which shows itself in different ways?

> Freda is well behind with her market research project. Her
> recent work has been hurried and careless. She looks tired and
> tense. Are her projects too demanding for her skills? Is poor
> sleep interfering with her work? Is her office sited so that she is
> distracted by casual callers? Does she have problems outside
> the office? Does she plan her work efficiently? Does she simply
> have too much work to do?

Any one of these problems could be the trigger. Identifying
it correctly is an essential step leading towards a solution.

Exploration is a mutual process

It is not enough for the manager alone to have correctly
defined the heart of the problem; it is important for the
presenter to have done so too. We all have a greater com-
mitment to the truths we have found for ourselves than to
those we have received – sometimes reluctantly – from
others. So the manager should prefer to provide a framework in which the presenter can do the discovering, rather
than eagerly using his superior wisdom to reveal the hidden
key.

This demands great self discipline from the manager. We
like to be asked to solve problems; the temptation to act the
guru is strong. And it is often reinforced by the presenter
who would prefer to be given the ready-packed solution
from on high than to go through the hard processes of

thought, and the discomfort of taking responsibility for his own answers. In fact, the manager is often better placed to understand the problem. His view is unmisted by emotional involvement; he will often be more experienced than the presenter; he may have met the problem before; he may even have been through it himself. But he must still hold back – giving the presenter the room to make his own discovery. When he asks a question, or suggests a line to explore, he must do so tentatively, leaving the presenter free to disagree or to verify the suggestion for himself. The manager's aim is to stimulate and guide the process of discovery, not to pioneer it.

For instance, a manager listening to the story of Charlie, the talented man who never seems to get anywhere, might so easily find himself saying:

> 'You do seem to have had a string of misfortunes, Charlie. But really, you know, you've only got one problem. You're the sort of person who gives up too easily – full of enthusiasm to begin with but, when the going gets tough, you just give up. What we've got to tackle is this persistency problem of yours.'

He's probably right, and Charlie may well agree. But suppose he tackles it differently:

> 'You do seem to have had a string of misfortunes, Charlie. It could just be a run of bad luck, but it might be worth our while trying to see if there are any common factors – sometimes that can give a clue to what's going wrong. Let's just run over the different incidents again, and perhaps you'd like to think whether they've got any features in common.'

This suggestion could lead Charlie to discover for himself the common source of his problems. And, if he does so, he will be more committed to making the changes which may be necessary.

Dangers of leading questions

There is a trap here. Questions which genuinely stimulate the presenter into finding the truth of the matter for himself are one thing; questions which are, perhaps unconsciously, designed to lead the presenter along a path towards the solution the manager already has in mind are another. Socrates, pretending to be a disinterested seeker after truth, followed this method; he ended up in the death cell. We should not be surprised: there is nothing more frustrating than being led, apparently with our freedom intact, into a conclusion with which we disagree.

> Katy is in hot water because she has failed to remind her boss of an appointment, having already mislaid an important file. Her boss is sure that Katy is a disorganized person – and that this is shown by her untidy desk. When he focuses her mind on this, and asks her whether she thinks that untidy people work in an untidy way, Katy finds herself agreeing that this must be where her problem lies.

Maybe so. But Katy has been steered into an admission, and may resent this – even though the solution may be correct. If her boss had merely told her his view, or even hectored her into agreeing, this might have been bearable. But his reasonableness and his gentle questions leave her caught on the wrong foot, without even the excuse to be angry about it.

The problem behind the problem

The core of the problem is often elusive. Both the presenter and the manager may be confident they know what it is, and yet be wrong. Perhaps, in the last example, both Katy and her boss are genuinely agreed that her disorganization is the cause of her mistakes – after all, it seems commonsense. But a more skilled boss would have wanted to explore the situation further – just to check if the first conclusion was correct.

> Gerald, a member of your staff, is about thirty. He does a good,

solid job of work in the marketing department. He is not very creative, but you have hopes that he will climb a rung or two further up the ladder. One disadvantage, which may hold him back, is that the marketing task is becoming more technical, and Gerald has no qualifications.

He comes to see you one day for a fairly substantial rise. He clearly feels strongly about this, and is a little nervous and emotional. He has brought his household budget with him to demonstrate that his current salary is insufficient for his reasonable needs.

What problem, or problems, would you pick out here, and where would you look for a solution? On the basis of the facts as presented, the problem is one of money, and the most likely solution is to encourage Gerald to obtain the qualifications which would justify a higher salary. But what you don't know, because Gerald hasn't told you, is that, a week or two before, a colleague of his – Robert - mentioned his salary in conversation. It was higher than Gerald's. Robert is about the same age and appears to Gerald to have equivalent responsibilities. The problem is not the absolute amount of his salary but the amount relative to Robert; it is not Gerald's sense of poverty which has brought him to you, but his sense of injustice. There may or may not be good reasons for the salary differential, but unless the situation is brought out into the open the real problem has not been recognized, and cannot be tackled.

It is easy to blame Gerald for this; he was holding back on information you could not have been expected to guess. But this may be to judge Gerald too harshly; perhaps he has really convinced himself that he is underpaid; his conversation with Robert may now be half forgotten, and he is not consciously aware of the part it is playing in his current feelings. And, whether it's Gerald's fault or not, the problem will still not have been solved; indeed time will probably be wasted following up a false trail.

Could you have been expected to have unearthed the Robert incident; after all, there may have been no clue? Provided that your exploration was open-minded, and not prejudiced by a premature analysis of the situation, it might have occurred to you to wonder what had started Gerald's train of thought. It could have been a number of things – some new expenses, a row with his wife about money – but in fact it was Robert. And, even if you had missed this question earlier, you might have had a second chance when you were sensitive enough – perhaps through observing his non-verbal communication – to realize that your talk about further qualifications was not meeting Gerald's need.

Who has the problem?

Part of finding the problem is establishing correctly with whom the problem lies. This is not always apparent at first sight:

> Evelyn, the manager of your print department, takes a great pride in getting the work completed on time. The new staff handbook has come out ten days late and Evelyn takes the delay very personally: it is her responsibility, her fault. Exploring the situation reveals that the personnel manager required a series of amendments right up to the last moment and, as a result, the work got out of schedule and had to wait until after the summer break.

It may be obvious to you that it is not Evelyn's fault – the personnel manager has the problem, which he has created for himself. But it is not obvious to Evelyn, whose temperament leads her to feeling that she is to blame for anything going wrong.

A manager may well feel that good exploration is a demanding task when even the presenter is laying, for the best of motives, false trails on the way to the truth. But a degree of benevolent distrust can be valuable in problem solving – particularly if you happen to be a sales manager:

> Looking at last quarter's figures the sales manager notices that, although sales in general have been good, Roger has reported figures well below the average for the group. At a subsequent meeting Roger explains that, although he has worked hard, his

results have been poor because the product is no longer competitive; his customers are buying elsewhere.

Over the years this sales manager has heard territory, advertising, sales promotion, the heat of the summer, the cold of the winter all proffered as reasons for poor sales results. In Roger's case he will be sceptical about lack of competitiveness when the rest of the team are doing well. The real reason may come out in exploration, but until Roger can realize that the problem lies with him and not with external circumstances the chances of constructive change are small.

The responsibility for change

Establishing with whom or what the problem lies should not turn into a fault finding exercise. Is it Katy's fault? Is it Evelyn's? Is it Roger's? Fault and blame are not very helpful words in the vocabulary of problem solving. They tend to be comments on the past, but the manager is only concerned with the changes which will improve the future. The positive question is: who has the responsibility for change? The answer to this is not necessarily the person who has the problem:

> Drake is in trouble with his budget submission this year. He has applied for funds to upgrade the computer equipment, and the firm's accountant has thrown out the expenditure as not being cost effective. Exploring the situation it appears that the difficulty does not lie in Drake's submission but in the accountant's lack of understanding of computers; this is made more difficult because the accountant is a hidebound person with little time for new-fangled ideas.

Without doubt the problem lies with the accountant. And this is where Drake feels the responsibility for change also squarely lies. But is this realistic? The accountant is not even aware that the problem exists, and he is unlikely to change the habits of a lifetime. Like it or not, Drake must assume the responsibility for change – if he wants to get his computer equipment. It is useless to waste thought and time wishing that things were different; what can be changed will be done through Drake's actions – and the next stage will be to decide what these should be.

Exploration should lead towards goals for change

The techniques used in the Exploration stage, examined in the next three chapters, will bring out more clearly how finding the core of the problem leads naturally into goals for change. Exploration is a stage in the LEGUP process, and its value lies in how well and how clearly it identifies just what and who has to change in order to reach a solution to the difficulty.

> As they explore the problem of Roger's poor sales results, he and his manager realize that the heart lies in Roger's poor technique for closing sales. He is letting his customers get off the hook too easily – leaving them easy targets for the next salesman prepared to push the issue to a conclusion.

Setting the right goals for change in this case may take a little time; but it is possible to see from the outcome of the exploration what these might be. The satisfactory completion of revision training in closing techniques might head the list, followed by Roger undertaking a target ratio of closes to sales interviews over the next quarter.

> When Drake realizes that he is only going to get his budget past the accountant by changing his approach, he wonders whether altering the presentation of his figures might help. His first goal might be to have a friendly chat with the accountant in order to establish just where the blockages lie. Then he will see if he can re-cast his figures, and supplement them with evidence in a form to which the accountant is more accustomed.

Summary

- The Exploration stage starts when the manager has a full picture of how the presenter sees and feels about the situation, and has reflected his understanding to the satisfaction of the presenter.

- The task of the Exploration stage is to explore the situation in order to identify the core of the problem so that possible goals for change may be established.

- This exploration should be mutual, and the manager's role is primarily to provide a framework which helps the presenter to examine the problem and to discover the truth.

- The real source of the problem may lie below the surface. The first solution should not be accepted too readily – even if the presenter is happy with it.

- Establishing who or what is the source of the problem is important; and the presenter must discover the degree and the nature of his own responsibility.

- While the presenter may not always have responsibility for a problem, he may have to accept responsibility for bringing about a beneficial solution. Problem solving is not a 'blame' game but a 'change' game.

6 Basic Exploration Skills

Exploration calls for the use of six basic skills as a foundation to the process: the use of creative questions to clarify and develop understanding; interpretive summaries which seek to reflect the deeper meaning of the speaker; the exploration of the feelings which have a bearing on the situation; ways of helping the presenter to express himself in concrete terms; the testing of possible courses of action for their consequences; and the provision of relevant information. These are looked at in detail; further, more specific, skills are examined in Chapter 7, and in Chapter 8 the Exploration stage is drawn together so that its relationship to the Goal setting stage may be seen.

In the last chapter I suggested that a problem, by the end of the Listening stage, was like a ball of wool left in the care of the cat. There are several tag ends – many which lead nowhere, and one or two which lead to unravelling. And that is the course which exploration usually takes. Asking questions which enable both the presenter and the manager to understand the situation more deeply, and following up the clues which may be spotted in the material given, make it possible to elucidate the confusion and to see the common factors which make sense of what has happened. A number of established skills have proved helpful in understanding problems, and in this chapter we will examine them. But a word of caution first. Skills are not an end in themselves; they are only methods of working – and they have to be used selectively. Because of your particular personality and way of working you will find some of them more valuable to you than others, and – just as important – you will need to choose the methods appropriate to the nature of the problem and to the nature of the presenter.

In order to study these skills in context I am going to provide a main background example which we will use throughout this chapter and the next. (Inevitably it will be somewhat artificial: no one, I hope, would want or need to use all these methods to solve one problem.) In reading the example try to pick out the points to which you would choose to return if you were carrying out the exploration.

A background example

Hal is a senior sales manager who reports to you. He is a very determined man accustomed to getting things done, and his sales team of thirty representatives performs extremely well. While you value him highly yourself, you know that his senior colleagues in the company resent his rather brusque ways, and his lack of concern about what he sees as bureaucratic detail. There may also be some envy because the bonus system you operate gives Hal a higher salary than his peers. The problem has come about because, quite late in the year, your budget controller has drawn to your attention the fact that expenditure in Hal's division is way over budget. This is rather serious because the company is short on working capital and, if costs are too high, the profits needed to service the company's overdraft, let alone to pay a decent dividend to shareholders, will simply not be available. The budget controller has recommended that Hal's expenditure for the rest of the year should be cut to the bone; and that some other projects – such as upgrading the computer system – should be postponed. What's more, the usual non-contractual bonus paid to all the staff at Christmas will need to be halved. The budget controller reminds you that this is by no means the first time that Hal has ended up over budget – though never so seriously as on this occasion.

Hal turns up for his meeting with you a few minutes late,

mentioning that he was caught on a telephone call to Copenhagen. But he wants to get down to discussion quickly, and you assume from his occasional glances at his watch that he is already thinking about his next meeting. You explain the situation to him briefly, showing the budget discrepancies; and you outline the budget controller's plan for rescuing the situation. By now Hal is beginning to look concerned; he has stopped looking at his watch. His first response is to demonstrate, with growing enthusiasm as he does so, the high sales results he has achieved; they are way over the forecast target and he is obviously proud of the leadership and teamwork which have brought this about.

When you mention the budget controller and his plan, Hal's mood changes; he moves back in his seat and a long-suffering expression appears on his face. In Hal's view the controller is a narrow sighted man, taken up with figures; if the sales go down but the books balance he's happy, but if they go up and throw out his calculations he panics. Is the company, Hal asks, to be run by accountants – or by businessmen? He then points out that far less money would be available to the company this year if his sales in previous years had not been so good. 'In any case,' he says, 'I've been over budget in previous years, and no one complained then. And anyhow, what's the budget controller been doing? It's now September, and if he'd been on the ball he could have spotted the problem at least by mid-year, and correction would have been far easier.'

As far as Hal's concerned, there can be no question of cutting back his budget. A few thousand here and now might be possible – though it would only be postponing expenditure – but serious pruning is out of the question. He has built up an enthusiastic team and to check them now, or deprive them of proper sales support, would be bad for morale. Even if no one resigned – and the market for good salesmen in this line of business is very competitive – it would be difficult, perhaps impossible, to get them back on song next year.

He finishes by pointing out that Chepstows and Siegfried Mansons, your two main competitors, don't seem to have any of these difficulties. They really back sales success. He knows this because Siegfried Mansons' managing director, with whom he was having a drink last week, was telling him about how they were putting big money behind the present sales boom; and he had even said to Hal that he didn't think his employers realized what a good man they had in him.

Asking questions

Perhaps the most commonly used tool of exploration is the question which clarifies an obscure or vague point, or which leads the presenter to think more deeply about what he has said. Hal has told you that there is no way in which his budget can be cut substantially without doing great harm. But at this stage you will not know whether he has already analysed his budget and arrived at this conclusion, or whether this is the immediate defensive reaction of an executive whose budget is threatened. You may, in fact, suspect that Hal is not particularly careful about budgeting, but you must leave him free to discover this for himself. Thus you would avoid a question like: 'How do you know, Hal, that you can't cut your budget? I've only just raised the point.' A better question might be: 'You mentioned just now that you couldn't cut your budget without doing great harm. Could we just look at your bigger expenditure items planned for the last quarter, and maybe you could point out to me which are the most important.' In answering that question Hal will quickly show whether he is familiar with his expenditures. If he is, the exploration could continue by trying to make a realistic assessment of how the different cuts might affect results. If he is not, you may be able to help him to see that his reaction was premature, and that he cannot really say that cuts are impossible until he has examined the possibilities in detail. Either way, you and he will have a better understanding of the situation.

You will notice that the question used is not in any way a trap: it does not push Hal towards a particular answer nor does it – whatever your private suspicions – assume what the answer will be. And it is not posed in a threatening way; exploration is not interrogation. Problem presenters are often inclined to be defensive, and any sense of being put on the spot rather than working mutually at the best solution will make the process more difficult. Rather, the question is *creative*; that is, it leads both of you onwards towards discovering the truth of the matter.

Some examples to test

Here are some examples of creative questions that might be used at the Exploration stage. Satisfy yourself that they observe the following three criteria:

1   They should be open questions which do not assume or indicate a 'correct' answer.

2   They should be posed in an exploratory and tentative way.

3   They should help the problem solvers towards a greater understanding.

'Penny, you tell me that the wolf whistles you get every time you go through the machine shop are really annoying you. But do you think, perhaps without meaning to, you contribute to it in any way – or would it not make any difference whatever you did?'

'You tell me you think that if we raised our prices by about 10 per cent our competitors would follow suit. But let's just suppose they don't, and we start losing market share – what would your contingency plan be?'

'If the company agreed to you taking over tinned soups as your principal product line, have you thought out your priorities? Where do you think you'd start?'

In each case the answer to the question may tell the participants some important things that go beyond the obvious answers – Penny may begin to examine whether her behaviour or her mode of dress has contributed to the situation; both of you will gain a better idea of whether the consequences of a price rise have been thought through thoroughly; you will discover whether the product manager is serious about the soups, or just wants a bigger job.

And there is of course the last and most useful question of all: '*why?*' 'Why do you think the budget controller is only interested in accounts and not in business success?' 'Why do you think your sales team has been particularly successful this year?' Remember the question 'why', and use it often.

Continuing creative questioning

One question leads naturally to another. We'll just take one of these examples, and imagine the exploration continuing:

Manager: If the company agreed to you taking over tinned soups as your principal product line, have you thought out your priorities? Where do you think you'd start?

Presenter: Well, I've been watching our product charts for a while now, and I've noticed that for the last year our soup sales in the West Country have been dropping. Getting those up to scratch again would be my first priority.

Manager: Why do you think sales have been falling in that particular area?

Presenter: Can't be sure at this stage. I'd have to talk to some of the customers first – and I'd find out what the competition's doing.

Manager: So it's market research first. And you'll really not know what needs to be done until that's finished?

Presenter: Yes, that's the way I'd work.

Manager: That makes sense. But, from what you've said, it looks as if you haven't yet done enough homework to know whether you could be really successful with tinned soups. Is that fair?

Presenter: Yes, I suppose that's right.

Manager: OK. Now, if you're asking me to give you this new product line I'll need something more than that to go on. How are you going to set about showing me what you think you'd actually do in order to increase sales?

Presenter: Hmm. I know we've got some market research on file; then I've one or two contacts in the trade who might help. Perhaps I ought to nose around a bit more. Mind you, I wouldn't want to produce a definite plan on that basis, but I think I could put forward some preliminary suggestions.

Manager: Now we're talking!

In that dialogue the manager, by use of creative questions, has enabled both of them to see that the presenter's application is premature since it is apparently based only on a general belief that he would succeed rather than hard evidence. And they have also established what has to happen in order to reach the next stage. Yet the manager himself has added very little new information; it was well chosen questions which helped the presenter to discover what had yet to be done.

Asking creative questions is an important management skill – and not only for problem solving. As usual, practice is essential. You may like to experiment with creative questioning over the next two or three days, and see how you get on. Your objective should be to see how successful you are in helping others to come up with good, well thought out decisions merely by asking the questions which help them to do so.

Interpretive summaries

In earlier chapters we looked at mirror summaries. And that's what they were: reflections, in the manager's own words, of what he had heard. The presenter was then able to see what he had said, and to modify or develop it. Interpretive summaries look behind the surface and attempt to reflect what the presenter really means. The manager is still not going beyond the evidence, so it's not guesswork; but, because the evidence is not always clear, interpretation is required.

'Hal, you've shown me your excellent sales results so far this year. I get the feeling from your manner that you're very proud of

what's happened. You seem to feel that all your previous hard
work has started to pay off. Am I right?'

In this instance the manager has picked up the enthusiasm in
Hal's voice and, we may guess, from his expression and his
gestures while he was retailing the results. You will notice
that the interpretation is tentative so that Hal can confirm or
deny it. If, for example, he replies: 'It's not the results I'm
proud of – it's my people: they've done the work', then he
has highlighted an important value for him which may have a
bearing on the eventual solution. Here, the manager has
brought into his summary the feelings which he believes Hal
has, and he bases this on what he has observed at one point
in the conversation. But it may often be appropriate to bring
together two or more parts of the conversation and to draw
an interpretive inference from these:

> 'Hal, you told me you were exasperated with the budget control-
> ler's preoccupation with keeping the books straight, and then
> you mentioned how our competitors back sales success. I'm just
> wondering whether you see the whole company as one which is
> a bit scared about getting out on a financial limb – not prepared
> to take business risks. Is that how you see it?'

In some instances you will have other information about the
individual or the circumstances which has not been mentioned in the interview, or may have come from a previous
discussion with the presenter. If relating that to the current
situation may throw light on it, then it should be brought in:

> 'I seem to remember, Hal, that you've crossed swords with the
> budget controller from time to time in the past and, from what
> you've just said, you haven't got a high opinion of him. Yet, as I
> recall, you got on fine with his predecessor. That suggests that
> it's more of a personality clash than anything else. Does that
> sound right to you – or is it something quite different?'

In these examples you may have noticed that the manager
presents the evidence for his interpretation. This allows the
participants to see whether it is justified. And the discipline

of evidence helps to ensure that the manager is not allowing his interpretation to be contaminated by his personal views.

Contamination of the interpretation

Interpretive summaries call for care and judgement. While they can be powerful ways of stimulating insights into the situation, they have their dangers. One of these is that it is only too easy to arrive at what sounds like an inference but which proves on examination to be simply a way for the manager to feed his own theories or assumptions into the picture. Supposing you had said:

> 'Hal, I just get the feeling from the way you dismissed the possibility of cuts in your budget that you're not really concerned about the company as a whole – provided you get your sales results. Have I got that right?'

you could expect a very negative reaction – and a bad outcome to the meeting. What you have suggested could be true, but you just do not have the evidence at this stage to support it. But even when you have kept to the evidence it is still possible to make a wrong interpretation. For instance, the suggestion to Hal that his difficulties with the budget controller are no more than a personality clash might prove incorrect. Some wrong interpretations are inevitable – and acceptable. But too many can damage the trust which is so important for problem solving, because they suggest to the presenter that you really haven't understood the situation well enough to be able to help. It can also happen that, although you have actually drawn the right inference, the presenter is not ready to accept it. This may be because he is too defensive, or because he has not yet realized the truth of what you are saying. But, however confident you are, avoid an argument. This only locks people into their position, and makes it almost impossible for them to change their view. It is better to move back, and approach another subject. You can always return to your suggestion at a later point – when you think the presenter may be ready to look at it with fuller insight. Even Hal might accept at a later stage that he often forgets about the company's broader interests in his eagerness to bring the sales in.

These dangers suggest that interpretive summaries should be introduced with care: care that they are really based on the evidence; care about choosing the point in the discussion at which to introduce them; and care about phrasing them in such a way that the presenter can deny or accept them freely. It is best to practise interpretive summaries in situations which are not sensitive. In this way you can assess how skilful you are, and how sure your instinct is, without risking serious harm.

Exploring feelings

I have already stressed that feelings, where problem solving is concerned, are facts – and need to be dealt with in just the same way as any other factor which has a bearing on the situation. Arguably they are often the most crucial element because they affect the way people see a problem, their capacity to be objective, and their readiness to bring about necessary changes. Hal provides a good illustration of this. He has feelings of pride about his team's results, feelings of dislike for the budget controller, feelings that he is undervalued and undersupported by his company. We know that no solution will really work if the feelings are working against it. Yet many managers are reluctant to deal directly with feelings. It may be, as some would claim, that they are hesitant to invade the emotional privacy of their colleagues; it may be that they personally find the whole area of feelings embarrassing, and therefore best avoided. But just as asking someone to take their clothes off might be frowned on in a factory but quite acceptable in a doctor's surgery, so exploring feelings in the context of problem solving face to face is often both appropriate and necessary; a manager must learn to do it well.

The exploration of feelings should only take place in a relationship where there is trust between the participants. To ask a man, for instance, how he feels about losing a promotional opportunity may seem an impertinence in the wrong atmosphere; while to ask him about his intimate marital affairs may seem quite natural and acceptable in the right atmosphere. The proper completion of the Listening stage is an important factor in setting up a trusting relation- ship, as I have explained (p. 31). But fine judgement will still be needed to ensure that the level of exploration always seems fitting to both parties. Secondly, exploration about feelings must be relevant to the problem being tackled. We have no business enquiring about feelings merely out of curiosity; and we should not be surprised if we get our noses bloodied when we do. The manager should always be able to demonstrate the relevance if the presenter asks him and, in sensitive areas, it is often helpful to volunteer the reasons why:

> 'Hal, it seems to me that you're always going to have problems if you keep scrapping with the budget controller. And maybe that won't be sorted out until you've got to the heart of the matter. It might help if you could explain to me just exactly how you feel about him – that could be a good starting point, couldn't it?'

That example also illustrates a third point: that humility is called for from the manager. Precisely because the presenter is being asked to reveal something which is normally private he needs to employ a tactful respect. And naturally it follows that sensitive information should be kept confidential – unless the presenter agrees otherwise.

Presenters may find it hard to express feelings

If managers sometimes find it difficult to ask about feelings, presenters can find it equally difficult to talk about them. This is not necessarily a result of reticence, but simply because they are not accustomed to it, and the vocabulary doesn't spring easily to mind. Yet a vague description of feelings may not be enough for useful work. Let's take the question to Hal about his feelings towards the budget con- troller a little further. See how the manager tries to bring some precision into Hal's expression of feelings.

Manager:...It might help if you could explain to me exactly how you feel about him – that could be a good starting point, couldn't it?

Hal: Well, it's nothing in particular. I just can't stand the man.

Manager: Yes, I think I've got that message! But tell me what you mean. It sounds as if you couldn't bear being in the same room with him.

Hal: Oh, it's not as bad as that. I'd never choose to spend time with him, of course; but provided we're not talking business I suppose he's OK.

Manager: So what happens when you talk business?

Hal: Honestly, you ought to hear him. He doesn't talk business at all – he talks computer print-outs. No matter what I try to explain he just comes back to his figures – either they add up or they don't. After a bit I feel my gorge rising.

Manager: So he just sticks to figures and won't listen to any other kind of argument. And that makes you feel sick.

Hal: Well, not sick perhaps. But I can feel myself getting angrier and angrier as he goes on.

Manager: So what do you do?

Hal: I used to lose my temper and give him a piece of my mind. Water off a duck's back! Nowadays I just make my excuses and leave – before I blow my top.

Manager: Sounds as if your meetings get you nowhere – in fact, they only make things worse.

Hal: That's right. So I now write him little notes instead – very polite, of course. He writes back: a four-page memo supported by appendices. Usually by then I've already spent the money, so I don't feel the need to read it.

Manager: So, if I've got you right, you don't care for him much – but you've got nothing against him personally. It's just that you find his narrow view of business so frustrating that you can't discuss things without getting mad. And now you've found a way of coping which avoids the issue altogether.

In that dialogue (in which, incidentally, you may have noticed that the manager was listening carefully, and giving mirror summaries) Hal has moved from '... nothing in particular. I just can't stand the man' to a clear expression of his feelings. We don't know how Hal and the manager will solve this difficulty, but at least they have concrete information from which to start.

Being concrete

As we have seen, it is important to be concrete about feelings, but helping the presenter to be concrete and specific about any of the points he is making may help you both to grasp the nature of the problem more clearly. You will have noticed that most of the points made in this book have been illustrated by one or more examples. I hope that this method has enabled you to grasp what I am trying to say in a very direct way. If I had merely described the points two things might have happened: first, your impressions would have been rather vague – you would often not have been sure exactly what I meant; second, I would not have been forced to think through each point clearly so that I could express it as an example.

In some instances I have omitted points because when I tried to put them into exemplar form they turned out to have no substance. I was, to put it another way, determined to make my points concrete, and to test their validity by doing so.

And, within the examples themselves, there have been several instances of the manager helping the presenter to turn what he is saying into concrete form. You may remember (p. 69) the product manager who wanted to be put in charge of tinned soups. Asking him to be concrete about what was currently lacking in the management of that line, and what action should be taken, led the product manager to see that he needed to do more research and planning before he could make a credible bid for the job. Concreteness about feelings has also been emphasized – thus Hal (p. 75) is helped to express his own feelings about the budget con-

troller, and, on the question of telling his team about redundancies if the cashflow problem is not contained, he is asked
(p. 78) to imagine himself actually making the announcement.

Concreteness can be very helpful in pinning down the
problem:

> **Manager:** You've told me that one of your printing machines is
> really out of date and no longer up to the job. But what exactly
> are the problems you're experiencing?
>
> **Printer:** The real trouble is that it's only a two-colour machine;
> we're getting more full colour work, and that means downtime
> to clean the rollers.
>
> **Manager:** Yes, I can see that's a nuisance. But how much time
> does it lose you in an average week?
>
> **Printer:** I should think only about three or four hours. But the
> real problem is that everyone wants their jobs done yesterday.
> I'm under a lot of pressure to speed up turnround.
>
> **Manager:** We're obviously going to need a new machine event-
> ually. But if we could wait till next year we'd save about £10,000
> in interest charges. What we've got to do is to weigh that against
> the inconvenience. I'll certainly investigate whether it's really
> necessary for everyone to require rush jobs, but do you think
> there's any way you can revise your workflow to relieve the
> pressure?

Presenters sometimes resist the request to be concrete. This
may be because they feel that it's not just the problem but
themselves who are being pinned down. Perhaps their points
will turn out to have no substance. In other cases they may
find it hard to articulate examples of what they mean, and
will require help to do so. But most often it is resistance to
the pain of sheer hard thinking. But hard thinking is the
essence of the Exploration stage, and it must take place if
problems are to be solved.

Consequence testing

Every manager knows that each action carries its consequences. While we may be able to alter situations a little to
suit the feelings and wishes of individuals, ultimately they
have to be faced. And it will often be necessary to ask the
problem presenter to look at the consequences of what he is
doing, or proposing to do. This is sometimes known as
reality testing, because it measures a course of action against
the reality of circumstances:

> 'Hal, being realistic, what do you think will happen if the com-
> pany does run out of cash and doesn't have the profit to service
> any more credit?'

> 'What would the consequences be if the directors accepted
> your suggestion – and left your budget intact while docking the
> staff bonus? What kind of cooperation would you get from the
> production and admin divisions next year?'

> 'Supposing you did join Siegfried Mansons, Hal – would it really
> solve your problems? In the end aren't they coping with the
> same market conditions as us?'

> 'How would you feel about explaining to your sales team next
> year that you were making some of them redundant because
> the company had to cut right back on sales for a while?'

Although these examples are in the form of questions, and
therefore allow Hal to agree or disagree, they are more
challenging than the other methods discussed in this chapter.
This means that they should be reserved until the process of
exploration is well established when manager and presenter
have built up a good understanding of their task, and have
passed beyond defensiveness into constructive exploration.
But, provided their basis is factual, a manager may owe the
presenter the opportunity to evaluate the consequences of
his actions. Reality must be faced, and the presenter will not
thank you afterwards for concealing it.

The last example – explaining to the sales team about

redundancy – takes us back again to feelings. Future feelings are consequences just as future happenings are. Since Hal has warm feelings of pride about his team, his ability to live with what may happen to them is important. He should not be deciding about a course of action until he has evaluated this as a factor in the situation. Imagining future feelings is difficult for most of us, and Hal may need some help. Sometimes a past incident can trigger the imagination – 'Remember when the Midlands branch was closed, and you had to let Fergus go. Would it be a bit like that?' – and sometimes the appeal to the imagination has to be direct – 'Imagine yourself standing up in the conference room and actually making the announcement. How would you feel then?'.

Giving relevant information

Although the presenter should be helped to take responsibility for solving the problem, this need not lead to the manager abrogating his responsibilities. Precisely because he is the manager he must be ready to make a direct contribution to the process by way of providing relevant information. He may be making this contribution at any point in the LEGUP process, except at the Listening stage, and it is likely to be important for effective exploration. We will glance briefly at some of the main headings under which this information might come.

The company and its structures

The manager must, by his position, interpret the company and its policies to his staff. A problem takes place within the context of an organization, and it must be solved within that context. The presenter needs to be aware of the ground rules, so this is information he needs.

'Hal, the company has recently conducted a review of its financial position and this revealed that we are in danger of running into liquidity problems through over-trading. It's been decided that the maximum growth in sales we can permit for the time being is

10 per cent a year. So in looking at this situation we have to bear that in mind.'

'You tell me, Hal, that you feel that the company is not really concerned to back your efforts. I think you should know that the whole subject was aired at length at the February board meeting. And the decision was that we should give sales the maximum support possible within the financial limitations, but that we must not do so at the expense of the production and administration divisions. You may or may not agree with that – but you can be confident that your needs were fully considered.'

'Yes, I fully understand how you feel about the budget controller. But he is specifically charged with monitoring and controlling budget variances. You may be able to get him to share your point of view – and that's fine. But there's no way I'm going to overrule a decision which is his responsibility.'

'Hal, I know you'd favour having the computer development work postponed in order to release more money for sales. I've considered that possibility, and I've decided against it. So the problem can't be solved that way.'

The last two examples illustrate the manager himself making a decision. While he is of course always free to decide how the whole problem will be solved, he will be reluctant to do so for the reasons I have given (see p. 21), and he will confine himself to setting out the limits within which the presenter can work. His responsibility is to communicate the bigger picture – the needs of the company as a whole, and how the problem and its solution fit into that.

Outside information

I have already warned you of the temptation the manager has to act the guru by using his superior knowledge to solve the problem before the presenter's eyes. But this danger should not preclude providing relevant information which will help the understanding of the problem. This might be information about the company's view, as in the previous examples, or of a more general kind:

> 'I wonder whether you've looked at Siegfried Mansons' last two or three annual reports, Hal. Their borrowings have been increasing substantially, and, reading their chairman's report between the lines, they're getting concerned about the level of costs. That may be worth bearing in mind when thinking about what their MD said to you.'

> 'Roger (p. 62), if you're getting plenty of sales interviews – and they're good quality – but you're not closing sales, you may be running up against a difficulty that many salesmen meet after a few years' experience. They feel they don't want to risk their relationships with customers by actively seeking orders. It seems more civilized to leave it up to them. Could that be happening to you?'

Reflecting reactions

This sort of information may be very relevant to the exploration of a problem, but it needs to be used with care because its effect is not always predictable. Used at the right stage, with the right person, it can be very effective:

> 'Hal, when we met this afternoon you gave the impression of being very busy. You told me you'd just come off an important telephone call, and you kept glancing at your watch. I got the message that you were really too busy, perhaps even too important, to spend time in conversation with me. Frankly that made me feel irritated, I found myself resenting you. I mention this simply because it may be that you have the same effect on other people. That's worth thinking about, isn't it?'

> 'Hal, when we were reviewing your monthly report at the board meeting someone noticed a couple of arithmetical errors. They weren't important, but I got the feeling from the directors that they thought you were a bit careless about your paperwork. Someone even made a joke about it. If that's their reaction

you're going to have to be very precise in documenting your
case for more money, don't you think?'

The value of reflecting your reactions, or the reactions of
others, lies in the fact that it's scarcely ever done. Most of
the time we're just left to guess about how people respond to
us – yet this may be very relevant to bringing about changes
in our behaviour. But the balance of risk must be considered: does Hal feel sufficiently secure in his relationship
with you to accept your feelings in the spirit in which you
presented them, and to respond constructively, or will his
sensitivity cause him to react negatively?

Interfering with the presenter's responsibility

The problem solving manager's preference will always be for
enabling the presenter to find out information for himself.
Thus it will be better if Roger can identify his reluctance to
endanger his relationship with his customers by himself, and
Hal might be asked to consider how someone might feel
about a person who constantly looked at his watch during an
interview. But when relevant information is not available to
the presenter it needs to be given. Exploration is not a
guessing game in which the manager knows certain facts but
is not saying. In trying to disentangle the problem the
presenter needs the best information he can get.

Practising the basic skills of Exploration

While the six skills involved have been seen in the context of
the Exploration stage plenty of opportunities to practise
them separately will arise in the course of your normal
management day. Chapter 1 suggests how this may be done.
But remember the cautions about appropriateness and relevance when you practise the examination of feelings.

Summary

- In the Exploration stage six skills are commonly used: asking questions, interpretive summaries, exploring feelings, being concrete, consequence testing, providing relevant information.

- Questions are used, not only to clarify obscure points, but as a way of exploring more deeply. Creative questions require the presenter to begin thinking the problem through constructively, and to obtain new insights thereby. They are not a form of cross examination, nor are they designed to elicit an answer the manager already has in mind; they are a mutual exploration of areas which may give or lead to an understanding of the problem, and who or what has to change in order to solve it.

- Interpretive summaries are made when the manager feels he can contribute to understanding by reflecting the insights he has gleaned. These are based on what has been said (or been shown through non-verbal communication) up to that point in the interview – and, often, from previous knowledge of the presenter and his circumstances. They should be suggested tentatively so that the presenter is free to confirm or deny. Good interpretations are helpful; poorly evidenced or inaccurate interpretations can inhibit the process.

- While some managers may be reluctant to explore feelings, their effect on the creation and resolution of problems is critical; therefore learning to explore feelings is a necessary skill for solving problems face to face. The technique should not be used until the manager is confident that the right level of trust has been achieved – and a good Listening stage will have helped in this. The exploration must be confined to the feelings relevant to the problem, and the manager should always be ready to explain the relevance. Since he is looking at an aspect which is often considered private, tact and respect are called for. Many presenters will find it hard to articulate their feelings, and so the manager must be ready to help them in this; until feelings have been identified with some precision it is difficult to know what part they play in tne problem.

- It is important to help the presenter to be concrete about his statements. Trying to express them precisely, perhaps using an example, sometimes reveals that they have no real substance. In other cases the process of making them concrete can help to pin down the problem in a way which allows it to be examined more effectively, and may indicate the next steps to be taken. Presenters sometimes find it difficult to be concrete, and may resist the process.

- A manager will use consequence testing to invite the presenter to measure a past or future course of action against the reality of circumstances in order to test the likely consequences. It can be quite challenging, and should therefore be used only when the manager has reason to expect a positive outcome. How one might feel in the future as the result of a proposed course of action is a type of consequence which presenters may find hard to visualize, and they will need help with this.

- The manager makes sure that the presenter has all the relevant information available; this may be about company policies and structures, managerial decisions, general information, or how others react to the presenter.

- All these methods are powerful, and the manager will need to practise them to develop his skills. There will be opportunities to practise them separately in the normal management day.

7 More Exploration Skills

Against the background of the basic methods described in the last chapter this chapter looks at a number of more specific skills that have proved useful as ways of examining aspects of a problem. Identifying patterns of behaviour may reveal how the presenter (or others involved in the problem) characteristically behaves – and thus give an opportunity for change. Similarly, presenters have certain attitudes of mind which affect their views and their actions; these need to be examined to see whether they help or hinder the situation. Presenters can often be helped to understand more of the elements in the problem by looking at it from the perspective of other participants, or looking at a similar problem in a different context. Sometimes the manager will become aware that parts of the presenter's account seem not to add up, or appear inconsistent; exploring this may well prove valuable – similarly the manager will be sensitive to significant remarks; these are often invitations, conscious or otherwise, for the manager to examine that area.

These behaviours may be thought of as clues (or tag ends in the ball of wool). By becoming sensitive to them, and skilful in following up, good progress in elucidating the problem may be achieved.

Consideration is also given in this chapter to using more than one interview for the Exploration stage (and the advantages which can be gained from this). The use of pencil and paper as an aid to exploration is discussed.

Patterns

During the Listening stage, or perhaps as exploration
develops, the manager becomes aware of a similarity between
a number of factors being described. At this stage he doesn't
know whether this is mere coincidence, but experience suggests that often, when followed up, it will prove to be the key
to the problem, or at least to part of it.

> Charlie (p. 56) has never got very far with his career, never
> written the book he's sure is in him, has been divorced twice.
> Each happening could be quite separate, and rationally
> explained. Or there may be a pattern here – perhaps one of lack
> of persistence. It's worth exploring.

> Three mornings out of five your secretary arrives late. This is
> annoying because you regularly need to work with her when you
> come in – before your first meeting. Her journey into the office is a
> notoriously difficult one because trains are frequently cancelled
> or held up. But you have also noticed that she is often late for
> meetings, and fails to get work done by deadlines. On every
> occasion you have questioned an incident she has a good reason.
> She is a truthful person, and you believe her. Is this just a run of
> bad luck, or is she contributing to her unpunctuality in some way?

> You have been discussing with Margaret the reasons for low
> productivity in her department. It turns out that there has been a
> good deal of minor illness, taking people away from work.
> Margaret is concerned about this and has satisfied herself that
> the illnesses are genuine. How can Margaret be blamed for the
> health of her staff? However, when both of you examine sickness
> records over a year or two you discover that the record has been
> generally poor, certainly significantly worse than the average for
> the company. This leads to a useful discussion about the possible
> reasons for this, including the level of motivation within the
> department – a factor for which Margaret may well have some
> responsibility.

> Peregrine, your branch manager in a large country town, has
> come in to talk over with you the poor standards he has been

experiencing from the head office service and administration departments. He has brought a file with him of long, carefully written memoranda he has sent. He tells you that people are very slow in replying, don't take his complaints seriously, or vaguely promise action, but do nothing. You are familiar with the memoranda: some of the complaints have been addressed to you, and arrive typed in red ink; but you have had copies of all the others because Peregrine believes in copying correspondence widely. In a sense Peregrine is presenting you with his pattern of behaviour, collected in a file. But has he asked himself how his addressees have come to look on his lengthy criticisms over the years, or how they react when they see the notorious red type waiting in their in-trays?

The patterns described in these examples are fairly obvious ones – particularly when a brief description shears them of the camouflage which prevents them being so easily spotted in real life. But in fact all of us, from temperament, upbringing, or learned habits have our characteristic ways of acting – patterns of behaviour which bring about a pattern of results. Of course these patterns can be helpful as well as damaging. For instance, I recognize that I become bored easily with routine, repetitive tasks, and tend to do them badly; I need the stimulus of novelty and mental challenge in order to be fully committed. That would be a bad pattern for certain kinds of jobs, but a good one for others.

Are there behaviour patterns in your own life?

So what about you? Looking at the patterns which operate in your own life can help you to understand what a strong influence they can be in the life of others. Quite trivial things – like whether you normally tackle difficult or easy jobs first, or whether you keep a clear or a cluttered desk – provide examples; so do rather more serious things – like why you have followed your particular career, or why you chose to marry a particular person. This is not just introspective curiosity; once you have recognized a pattern it is possible to judge whether it is helpful or not. And having judged, you can consider whether and in what way you should change –

or, if change is impossible, how you might adapt your life so that you maximize on a useful pattern and minimize on a destructive one. This is a form of internal problem solving, and exactly the same principle operates in solving problems face to face – look at what is happening, consider whether there is a pattern involved, think about how that pattern may be changed.

For example, Margaret – once she has recognized that sickness in her department is a pattern rather than an isolated bad patch – is able to look at the reasons. It might be poor work conditions, or simply that the routine of the department is very boring. Perhaps her staff have never seen how their work fits into the enterprise as a whole. Perhaps Margaret is given to taking correct work for granted, is hard on mistakes but gives no praise for success. Or perhaps she, too, is given to taking time off frequently for sickness. The last two possibilities constitute patterns in themselves; this time, patterns of Margaret's behaviour.

You may like to look back now at the description of the interview with Hal, the sales manager (p. 65). See if you can spot any possible patterns which might be worth exploring.

Exploring patterns

Hal gets on badly with the budget controller; he also has a history of friction with other senior colleagues. Is there a pattern here? Could it be usefully pursued, or is it too sensitive for that? An easier pattern to deal with is the one suggested by the remark that Hal has been over budget in previous years. Because Hal has said this himself it can be more easily opened up for examination. The dialogue might go like this:

Manager: Hal, I'd just like to go back to a remark you made earlier. You mentioned that this isn't the first year that you've ended up over budget.

Hal: That's right. And no one's made any fuss about it before; I just don't know why it's all blown up this time.

Manager: D'you think it's possible that that might be the cause? People might have built up the impression that you don't take a lot of notice of budgets – and that makes them quicker to react when they think the excess is really going to cause a cashflow problem?

Hal: It's possible, I suppose.

Manager: Would it be fair for them to see you like that?

Hal: No, of course not. I only spend what I absolutely have to. You know how sales have boomed this year. And last year we had to bump up our advertising to match Chepstows, or we'd have lost market share.

Manager: OK, I accept that. But I seem to recall, without checking, that your budgets ended up wrong for a year or two before that. Is that right?

Hal: Well, maybe. Yes, I expect so – but there were good reasons.

Manager: I don't doubt that for a moment. Certainly no one's suggesting – least of all me – that you don't get the best out of the company's money. But looking at it as a whole – you seem to come out well above budget four years out of five. That suggests that something's going wrong somewhere. Taken separately I'm sure there's always a good reason – but four years out of five sounds like more than a coincidence.

Hal: I can see it must look like that; but what are you really getting at?

Manager: I'm not sure. It could easily be that you've just had a run of bad luck – things have cropped up that no one could be expected to foresee. But I wonder whether that's the real explanation. Another possibility is that you haven't been very accurate in predicting market change. Or possibly you've not exercised proper controls over expenditure, so that it's always rising above forecast. Or maybe there's a bit of you that's tempted to say that getting accurate budgets isn't all that important – if the market's there the company will find the money.

Hal: Well, it certainly doesn't look like just bad luck – four misses out of five sounds like bad shooting. But no one can fault me on market changes – I guess I'm as accurate as anyone. There might be something in your last point, though. It's nothing like the whole explanation, of course – the market is so very volatile. But it does always seem a bit pointless to me going through a huge forecasting exercise when in the end I'm going to have to spend what's needed to grow our market share.

Through being asked to look at the pattern of budget performance rather than at each year separately Hal has had to face up to the real possibility that the difficulty is, at least to some extent, of his own making. By itself this will not solve the problem but it helps to build up the whole picture. You will have noticed that the manager leaves Hal quite free to maintain that it is simply coincidence – there is no accusation here, only an invitation for him to review the possibility of a pattern.

Experienced problem solving managers become very acute in spotting possible patterns. They have learnt that they have so often proved the key that it is always worth while checking to see if something similar has happened before. Even at the Listening stage, when they are not consciously analysing the material, their mental cash registers will ping when something that sounds like a pattern begins to emerge. At the Exploration stage they have to decide whether to follow it up – and when. It is easy to see, for example, that Hal could easily have interpreted the dialogue above as an attempt to prove him wrong, unless the manager introduced the idea at the right time. But there are other occasions when clear patterns can be presented right at the beginning of the Exploration stage, and result in coming close to the source of the problem very speedily:

Manager: Jim, I've been looking through your sales records. There may be an interesting point here. You close a lot of sales with firms where the buyer is a man, but very few when it's a woman. Does that give us a clue?

Jim: I've never really thought about it. I get on pretty well with women on the whole. But there must be something I'm getting wrong – my attitude, I mean. I wonder what it can be.

Manager: I've been wondering about these faulty batches, Jennifer. Have you noticed they most often occur on Wednesdays? What is it about Wednesdays in your area?

Jennifer: Nothing, really. The only thing I can think of about Wednesdays is that it's the head of departments meeting. Oops! That might be it. I never manage to see the Wednesday morning batches before they go out.

Questioning assumptions

The general assumptions we make about life are closely related to patterns of behaviour. Indeed they are often the cause. In the case of Jim, above, who has difficulty making sales to women buyers, we might imagine that further exploration revealed that he found it difficult to see women in an executive capacity, and that his lack of respect for their status led him to treat them inappropriately. In fact, of course, we all make assumptions because we have to; they are prepackaged judgements that experience has taught us are useful. For instance, I would readily assume that a new product will always cost more to produce than expected, and that computer programs will never work the first time. Many assumptions are made about classes of people – older people won't accept new ideas, Italians are emotional, long-haired youths are layabouts. We also make them readily about individuals – Elsie never completes a job on time, Andrew has no ambition, Pip's an ideas man, but he's not practical. Sometimes we can cite evidence for the assumption: perhaps Elsie has been behind with so many projects that there is every reason to expect that she will continue to be. But although assumptions are useful – and to some extent inevitable – they are also dangerous. Sometimes they are based on insufficient evidence: maybe we assume that Pip is not practical merely because we believe that ideas men always have their heads in the clouds. Sometimes the situation changes: Andrew may not have been ambitious when he was a bachelor, but perhaps his marriage has altered that. Sometimes we don't allow for the exceptions: the older men who welcome new ideas, the hippy who works in a children's home. It would be easier if we were always aware of the assumptions which lie behind judgements; then there would be a chance to reconsider and correct them. But the trap lies in the fact that they are often unconscious. And it is worth bearing in mind that each manager brings his own assumptions into the problem solving process; thus Katy's manager (p. 58) assumes that an untidy desk means an untidy mind. He may or may not be right but unless he is aware that he makes the assumption he cannot check it.

The problem solving manager will try to understand the unconscious assumptions on which the presenter appears to be acting. And he must be ready to help the presenter verify these if it seems they may be contributing to the problem. Hal could be making a number of such assumptions, and you may like to refer back (p. 65) to see how many you can spot. Here is a brief list; you may be able to find more:

- He believes that the best way to get things done is to be brusque.

- He believes you will be impressed because he has been held up by an international call.

- He believes the budget controller is preoccupied by figures.

- He believes that the company will always find the money to support his sales success.

- He believes that other functions in the company should be subsidiary to sales.

- He believes his sales team would not accept the need to cut back for a period.

- He believes that competitor firms would give him better support.

We don't know from the evidence available whether Hal is actually making all those assumptions, but there is reason to suppose that he may be. Some may be correct and useful; others are marginal to the problem and would therefore be disregarded in practice. But assumptions like the belief that there will be unlimited financial support for his sales or that his salesmen would walk out if they were asked to cut back for a period might be usefully explored. There are a number of different ways to help people review their assumptions – good, creative questions, for instance:

> 'Hal, I take your point – the company wouldn't have any income at all if your sales team didn't get it for us. But then what would your salesmen have to sell if we didn't have a production department to make the goods, or a despatch department to deliver them? Which comes first, the chicken or the egg?'

or interpretive summaries:

> 'You've told me you don't like beating about the bush, Hal, and you've quite often been pretty direct with me. It sounds as if you think that's really the only way to get things done. Is that how you see it?'

But it is the sensitivity of the manager to the possible assumptions being made by the presenter which comes first. Sometimes they are spotted as soon as the Listening stage is completed. In giving mirror summaries the manager has momentarily to adopt the presenter's perspective, and therefore his assumptions. For instance, in reflecting Hal's belief that competitor firms like Chepstows or Siegfried Mansons would give him better support than his own company, the sensitive manager would notice that Hal may be making the assumption that the grass is always greener on the other side of the fence; and he would store this mentally for possible exploration later.

Changing the frame of reference

This is a very powerful method which, used appropriately, can often unblock a difficult Exploration stage. Here are two examples of its use:

> 'Hal, just suppose for a moment you are a clerk in despatch department. You've worked pretty hard this year, always willing to get those rush orders out on time, and so on. Then round about the first of December, when you and your wife have made plans for the family Christmas, you get a note from the personnel director which says that the usual bonus has been slashed by 50 per cent. When you make a few enquiries you discover it's because sales expenditure is well over budget, and the cash is simply not available. How exactly are you going to feel about that?'

> 'Let's imagine, Hal, that you are the budget controller sitting in my office right now. And I've asked you to describe that last meeting with Hal, the sales manager. How would you describe it?'

Resistance to changing a frame of reference

The presenter is being asked to lay aside his own perspective, and to see matters from another point of view. This is not an easy thing to do: you will remember that the manager has to go through this process as part of learning to listen well. And a problem presenter like Hal may have a vested interest in not seeing another's point of view. He may resist, not by refusing to answer but by doing so on his own terms:

> **Hal:** Well, of course that budget controller would give you a completely different story. I've already said he's blind to anything except figures – he couldn't tell you anything useful.

> **Manager:** I don't suppose he'd actually come in here and tell me he had nothing useful to say because he's blind to anything except figures! But tell me what you think he actually would say. How would he put it?

Hal: I just don't know. I mean, I'm not him, am I?

Manager: No, of course not. But just imagine you were him – seeing the situation through his eyes and background. And here am I saying: Tell me about the meeting with Hal when you last discussed his budget? Now, what would you answer?

Another form of resistance is to avoid taking the question seriously. For instance, asked about the despatch clerk learning of his reduced bonus Hal might answer perfunctorily 'I guess he'd be pretty angry', and then try to change the subject. But the manager may want to push the point more firmly:

Manager: So he'd be pretty angry. What d'you think he'd say about it to his colleagues in the canteen at lunchtime?

Hal: I hate to think. I suppose he'd call the company mean – only he'd put it more strongly than that.

Manager: I bet he would. And what would he say about sales?

Hal: He'd blame us, of course – people always do. I think I'd keep my BMW out of the car park for a few days – I don't fancy any scratches.

Manager: So you reckon he'd be very angry – and want to take it out on sales because he'd assume it was all their fault?

Hal: Yes, I guess so. That's how I'd feel if I were him.

Changing the frame of reference is a versatile method

In that last answer Hal encapsulates the process of changing a frame of reference. Before the dialogue he was only open to his own point of view – ignoring or dismissing the other people affected by his actions. Now that he has made an imaginative leap into their frame of reference there is a much better chance that he will be able to explore the problem more objectively. Of course such a method can be very valuable in many different problem settings:

A member of your staff has been asked to give a talk to the

Chamber of Commerce in his local town, on the subject of why the company is opening a second branch in the high street. He is not an experienced speaker and he has asked you for help. You suggest that he asks himself what a member of the audience will be hoping to learn from the meeting, and not just what he feels he ought to say. By asking him to consider the audience's frame of reference he is able to develop ideas for a successful speech.

In a proposed company reorganization Lilian has been offered new duties which she is unhappy about. She is rather depressed and negative, and she wants to see the personnel director and tell him so. It is the personnel director who has planned the reorganization, in which Lilian is a key figure. You ask her to tell you what she thinks the personnel director is likely to feel about the reorganization, and how he will react when she announces that she's unhappy about her role. In doing so she realizes that he is likely to be touchy about it, and perhaps annoyed by either having to re-work it or accept that Lilian will be unmotivated in her new job. And so she decides that she will set out her ideas of how she can contribute effectively but in a way which she would enjoy doing. She will still tell him that she doesn't like what is currently proposed, but she will also offer him a positive alternative.

Unpopular management decisions

Changing a frame of reference can be a good way of handling unpopular management decisions. It needs to be used sparingly to avoid possible resentment, or the suspicion that you are abrogating your responsibilities.

'Just imagine for a moment, Hal, that you were in my situation. You've received a strict instruction from the directors that the cashflow limits must not be exceeded. In front of you is a sales manager who tells you that sales will fall back if his budget is cut. Tell me, what decision would *you* make?'

'Jennifer, you've made a very good case for taking over sales promotion department, but so has Francis. Now just stand back for a minute – forget your own point of view, and look at the company's. What do you think would really be the best decision for everyone in the long term?'

You may think this is unfair since it risks asking someone to argue against their own interests. For this reason I only employ it in moments of desperation – which is more often than I would like.

The vivid analogy can help

Another variation is to take the problem presenter right out of his immediate context so that he can see it with entirely fresh eyes. For instance, you might ask Hal to consider how you decide priorities in a household budget when it's a choice between buying a bargain this week and having enough cash for the bills due next week. Hal may, like most of us, be so wrapped up in the importance of business that he forgets that the principles are very simple; and such an analogy brings the problem down to the personal scale where the principles are easy to see. Or:

> 'Yes, I can see, Mr Brown, that setting up a market intelligence department would be quite costly; and I also appreciate that, at least in the short term, it won't contribute to profits. But think of it like a general sending a scouting party ahead of his troops. They're able to spy out the land ahead – and the enemy movements. Without them he'd never be able to prepare for the nasty surprises nor for the opportunities to take the new territory over the hill. If you were the general would you prefer to have scouts, or to take a chance?'

But this method has been in use for a long time:

> In the second Book of Samuel we read how King David, notwithstanding his harem, seduces Bathsheba the wife of Uriah, one of his liege men. Later he arranges for Uriah to be exposed to great danger in battle so that he is killed. Nathan, the prophet, wishing to change David's frame of reference, tells him about a rich man with great flocks who arranges for the only possession

of a poor neighbour, a little ewe lamb, to be stolen:

'And David's anger was greatly kindled against the man; and he said to Nathan, As the Lord liveth, the man that hath done this thing shall surely die. And Nathan said to David, Thou art the man. And David said unto Nathan, I have sinned against the Lord.'

We might hesitate to follow Nathan right the way through since his next announcement is that David's small son will die, and this will be his punishment – a managerial measure which is probably against the Employment Acts. But it is a dramatic example of enabling someone to see a situation in an entirely new light.

Inconsistencies

Our experienced listener (at the beginning of Chapter 4) mentioned inconsistencies as an example of the kind of thing which pinged in her mind like a cash register, and which she would store for future use. They are not always easy to spot since they are rarely obvious, but it is usually worth investigating anything which doesn't seem to the manager to add up. In Hal's case a possible inconsistency lies in his remark that the budget controller should have spotted his budget overrun by mid-year and not left it until September. Here the manager might want to ask Hal to consider how reasonable it was to expect the budget controller to spot an obvious discrepancy earlier than the executive who is running the budget in question. This could lead to a valuable discussion about budget responsibility.

You may have spotted another inconsistency in the original account of the discussion – which the manager might raise with Hal in this way:

'There's one point, Hal, I'm not clear about. You were showing me your very excellent sales figures a few minutes ago. Yet when you were telling me about your chat with the managing director of Siegfried Mansons you were implying that there was a general market boom which all our competitors are enjoying, too. Are we just sharing in the same boom as everyone else, or have we actually done better than the others?'

Sales people are (and perhaps should be) natural optimists, accentuating success and minimizing failure. And that makes it all the more important to explore the reality of the situation when management decisions are being made or, as in this case, there is an implication that special consideration should be given because of success.

Challenging inconsistencies may uncover surprises

Inconsistencies are, in a way, the reverse of patterns, and can be just as revealing. But often the revelation can be a surprise – leading the manager to understand a person or a situation better than he did before:

Manager: Petra, you were telling me the other day that you weren't being kept fully occupied, and that you could handle a lot more typing than you get at present. Now you're asking me if we'll buy you a word processor. I don't quite see how that adds up; I could see the reason for a word processor if you had too much typing, but not if you have too little. Have I missed something?

Petra: Yes, it's not like that at all. What happens is that a lot of the work is reports and sales promotion copy. It's the sort of stuff that needs endless alterations as different people review it at each stage. So naturally it gets sent to Central Secretarial because they use word processors. The girls there complain that they're overworked, while I'm twiddling my thumbs. With a word processor I'd get that work given to me. Central Secretarial would be delighted, and I wouldn't sit clock watching half the day.

Inconsistent behaviour

The inconsistency spotted by the manager may not be confined to what has been said; inconsistent behaviour can also be relevant:

'Hal, there's just one point I'd like to check out with you. You seem to be very much against the company imposing too much control on your budget. Yet you have the reputation of being very tough about your salesmen's expense accounts. At first sight I don't see how the two go together. Can you explain?'

Tact

Checking inconsistencies clearly requires tact in order to avoid implying that the presenter has been caught out in an untruth. And few of us, despite Emerson's view ('Foolish consistency is the hobgoblin of little minds'), like to be accused of inconsistency. But, in the examples above, you will notice that the manager explores on the assumption that the inconsistency arises from his misunderstanding of what has happened, and that it can easily be reconciled. Freed from any pressure to defend himself the presenter is able to review the apparent inconsistency objectively.

Significant omissions

'Is there any other point to which you would wish to draw my attention?'
'To the curious incident of the dog in the night-time.'
'The dog did nothing in the night-time.'
'That was the curious incident,' remarked Sherlock Holmes.

Significant omissions occur when the presenter doesn't say what we would have expected him to say. Like Sherlock Holmes, in 'Silver Blaze', the manager must examine the significance of what is not said, just as he would examine what is said. The account of the Hal interview does not reveal any very obvious evasions, but we might wonder why Hal throws all his defence against the cuts on his budget, and omits any reference to the postponement of the computer system upgrade – which could eventually affect the sales service, or the halving of the staff bonus which, as we have seen, could lead to poor cooperation from others. At the least this would confirm the impression that Hal thinks on a very short term basis (another assumption worth investigating?) and does not easily think about the long term or broader consequences of his actions.

A clearer example might be provided by Dennis, a man in his middle years who told his manager that the hospital specialist had asked him to undergo a course of treatment which would require him to attend hospital every second day for a period of several weeks. Dennis was very optimistic about the situation, although the treatment was going to be a painful one. His manager noticed that Dennis made no reference to how his work would be affected – yet Dennis could scarcely have helped wondering how his boss would react to such a prolonged series of absences. So this seemed worth exploring:

Manager: I don't envy you Dennis, it all sounds most demanding. Still, if it's really going to put things right, it'll be well worth it. But tell me, you've got a key job in your department – you haven't mentioned your thoughts about how the work will be covered.

Dennis: (rather hurriedly) Oh, that'll be looked after, don't worry about that. We'll manage.

Manager: Be sensible, Dennis. We want you back fit and well – and that's not going to happen unless you've got proper coverage. You're too important to us to let any concern about the job being done properly interfere with your concentration on getting well.

Dennis: (sitting back in his chair, relaxing) I have thought about it, actually. Sandra hasn't been with us that long but she's learning very fast. It might be an opportunity for her to take some more responsibility.

Manager: That sounds a good idea. Have a word with Sandra – if she's keen, why don't we ask her to take over some of your duties on a strictly temporary basis. I'll keep an eye on her myself. But you'll have to promise only to take on the jobs you can really cope with until you're fully fit.

In this case nothing would have been served by challenging why the point was omitted. Dennis clearly showed through his non-verbal communication that he was worried about keeping his job. Once reassured he was able to deal with the situation constructively. In another instance it might be necessary to challenge directly:

> A machine worker has approached you during your daily tour of the factory and has explained to you a useful idea which would enable a rather expensive process to be cut out altogether. Throughout the conversation he never mentions his section leader, who happens not to be at work that day. When you ask him why he hasn't told you about the section leader's reactions he mumbles a bit. Pressed a little, he explains that the section leader is a very strong union man, and would certainly quash any idea which could lead to a reduction of work. That's why he has approached you directly. Armed with this understanding you must now find a way of investigating the idea without making the machine worker unpopular with his boss or other colleagues.

Significant remarks

Occasionally what appears to be an omission is accompanied by a significant remark. Calman, the cartoonist, has a husband saying to his wife: 'What do you REALLY want?' And she replies: 'I want you to know without my telling you.' Presenters sometimes want managers to explore an aspect of the problem without having to raise it themselves. An example of this is the story of Ferguson (p. 35), who approached his MD ostensibly on the subject of a subordinate's promotion – hoping it would lead to a discussion of his own advancement. And they will often throw out a clue at some point in the conversation which, consciously or unconsciously, they are hoping you will pick up. The machine worker, in the account above, might well have remarked, apparently casually, and maybe with humour: 'Of course ideas aren't good news around here.' His hope would be that you would pick this up, question it – and thus take responsibility for obliging him to tell you that his section leader was against labour saving ideas.

> Andrea, who is on your public relations staff, is discussing an opportunity for promotion to a post which will oblige her to spend occasional nights away from home. She has not been married long and, if she had failed to mention her husband's reactions, you would have regarded that as a significant omission. But Andrea – whose pride in her independence would stop her raising the subject directly – is not prepared to rely on your sensitivity to pick up the subject. And so she works into the conversation the remark 'It'll be good for John, too – absence makes the heart grow fonder,' and then moves the conversation on. Having noted the remark you allow an interval to elapse and then return to it: 'You said just now that absence makes the heart grow fonder. Does John agree with that?' Invited to comment, Andrea reveals that she hasn't discussed this with John yet, and she is nervous about his reactions. This gives you both a chance to explore how the subject might be raised, and for Andrea to consider how she might respond to John's possible feelings.

Significant remarks are also made unintentionally. For instance, we do not have to assume that Andrea's remark about absence was deliberate; it may just have slipped into her conversation because the subject of her husband was on her mind. Or we could imagine Hal making a disparaging remark about staff in relation to the Christmas bonus which was significant of an underlying attitude of which he was not himself conscious.

Successive interviews

A number of problems a manager will face cannot be dealt with adequately at one session. Sometimes the amount of time available precludes this, and it is always better to propose a further meeting than to hurry a problem to a quick conclusion. But there can also be positive reasons for having more than one session: problems often benefit from the participants having the opportunity to mull over the stage they have reached. They may need to examine new insights, or to have the chance to review what they have said and perhaps to revise it. Thus Hal might come back on a second occasion and tell you that, looking back, he feels he's been a bit hard on the budget controller; he's even remembered an occasion when the controller went out of his way to support him when Hal wanted to finance a new branch operation.

The need for homework

One of the most common reasons for taking one or more sessions to deal with a problem is the need to do 'homework' in between. The product manager (p. 69) who discovered that he needed to research the tinned soup market before coming up with plans for improvement would need time to do this. And one can imagine Hal accepting the suggestion that he should spend some time studying his budget in order to consider what cuts might be possible, and in what order of priority.

It is very much within the spirit of good problem solving that much of the work should be done by the presenter in between sessions; the manager then becomes a facility for reporting and discussing progress – followed by planning the next moves. As we shall see in the later stages of problem solving (the Pursuit stage) intervals can be a necessary part of the process.

The manager's homework

The manager may have some homework to do, too. If time is not to be wasted at successive sessions he may find it valuable to complete some rough notes following each interview. This is usually best done almost immediately – perhaps keeping a special tape on a dictating machine for the purpose. He will then be able to review the notes before the next meeting, not only to remind himself of what was said but also to consider where he may usefully guide the coming discussion. There may also be points he has not yet had time to explore – perhaps a possible pattern or a significant remark – and he is unlikely to remember these without a note. He will also need to note any tasks he or the presenter has agreed to carry out before they next meet. A secondary advantage is psychological: the problem is uniquely important to the presenter, but only one among many concerns for the manager. Being able to demonstrate that he has remembered what was said and where they had left the problem last time will be seen by the presenter as further evidence of care – even if he is aware that the manager keeps notes. Of course, notekeeping can seem a chore. I suspect that once Hal had left the room I would be only too keen to get on immediately with something completely different. Yet in the long run it is well worth the discipline – to increase the efficiency of problem solving, and to save time overall.

Pencil and paper

At the end of the Listening stage the problem presenter may have produced quite a bundle of information, thoughts and feelings. The task of the Exploration stage is to try to make sense out of this, and to identify the core of the problem. But often the problem will become even more complicated at the early stages of exploration: the presenter, stimulated by the discussion, will think of additional points; and this may be further complicated when different ways of looking at the several aspects of the problem are examined. It can be helpful to use a pencil and paper (or whiteboard or whatever) to put the points down in a way which reminds both manager and presenter of what is going on, and to help them to see the problem as a whole. It can be a useful method of recapitulation enabling the participants to review the process, and sometimes to spot central elements in the problem which had escaped their notice before. It can also be valuable for occasions when the presenter is inclined to go round and round in circles – re-visiting earlier material but not taking it any further. When the information is down on paper it is easy for the manager to point out which ground has already been covered, and to urge the presenter forward into new investigation.

Some managers prefer to list the main points, but others

find that problems tend to be too diffuse to be easily reduced to a list, at any rate in the early stages. They prefer to use a diagram which corresponds more closely to the way the problem had been presented. This diagram can be easily added to, although it may be necessary to produce successive amended versions as further insights are gained.

A manager might, or might not, choose to use such diagrams when dealing with the problem of Hal. But because it is one we have followed through in some detail I have sketched out an example of the sort of diagram which might have been used (Figure 7.1). Your first reaction on seeing the completed diagram may be that it is even more complicated than the problem! But you must recall that it would have been built up, almost at random, from the central fact, SALES EXPENDITURE IS OVER BUDGET, by Hal and the manager together. For instance, BUDGET CONTROLLER is identified as a central factor – and his presence on the paper gives rise to a number of additional points which may be important. Similarly, on the left-hand side where the proposed solutions are listed, the drawbacks of each solution can be added as they come to mind.

When they review the diagram together it is clear to Hal and his manager that the most important area is COMPANY'S POSITION. The other elements are important – some more so than others – and will have to be taken into account if any solution is really going to work. But everyone's future depends on the company being able to continue trading and therefore the different ways in which this might be ensured must be considered first. These can then be examined in the light of other important factors, and the best means chosen. But clearly, even if an immediate solution is discovered, the difficulties will continue to arise if no way is found to match Hal's sales costs against available cashflow. Thus they use the diagram to consider where they are, and what the next steps in their exploration should be.

This method of drawing order out of complexity by using a chart which grows outward from the centre is fully described by Tony Buzan in *Use Your Head* (see bibliography). It is

Figure 7.1   Hal's problem

the single most valuable thinking tool I have ever encountered. Of course each manager will develop his own methods
of using paper and pencil – and there is a great variety of
possible ways, of which the following are only a sample:

- Establishing the presenter's order of preference: ask
  him to list, say, the five aspects of his job he values the
  most in any order; then ask him to knock out the three
  least important.

- A presenter is a little nervous or confused: ask him to put some notes on paper of the next point he wants to make; being able to work in his own time, and not meeting you eyeball to eyeball, may unblock him.

- Work with the presenter to make a pros and cons list, and then assess the balance. See also the PUSH-MEPULLYOU diagram in Chapter 10.

- Understanding how the component parts of a process, or functions in an organization, work together by drawing a diagram showing connecting lines. An example appears in Figure 9.1, where Benedict and his manager are trying to clarify his goal strategy. See also Figure 8.1.

Practice

Following my suggestions in Chapter 1 about ways of studying this book I have reminded you from time to time of the need to put what you have read into practice in an organized way. Here is an example of a manager practising two of the skills described in this chapter on an informal occasion:

Over lunch a colleague mentions that a valued member of his staff is leaving the company. You are aware that he has had similar losses in the recent past. To practise exploring patterns you say: 'You seem to have taken quite a bashing over staff leaving recently – have they all done it for quite different reasons, or is there any common factor?' Your colleague believes that it is simply a question of the higher salaries being paid elsewhere. However, later in the conversation, he says that although staff losses are a nuisance he is not finding it hard to replace with well qualified personnel. Spotting a possible inconsistency you say: 'I don't quite see how that works out. If we're paying the competitive salaries which attract new staff, how come we're losing existing staff because our salaries aren't high enough?' In exploring this it appears that other companies are offering more challenging opportunities than you are, and the conversation moves usefully to discussing what might be done about this.

Summary

Within the basic skills used for the Exploration stage a number of methods have proved valuable in helping to identify the key elements in the problem:

- Patterns: the participants notice that there seems to be a common thread between incidents presented at the interview, or when related to previous happenings. Investigating this may show that a characteristic pattern of behaviour is responsible – thus giving an opportunity to modify one factor which can benefit several aspects of the problem.

- Assumptions: presenters, like all of us, make certain assumptions about life, about people in general, and about particular individuals. Sometimes these assumptions can be incorrect or inappropriate, and thus be contributing to the problem. Because the presenter may be unaware of his assumptions the manager must help him to find and examine them.

- The frame of reference: it is hard for people to escape from their own frame of reference and to see a problem from a different point of view. Understanding will often be accelerated when the presenter is able to put himself into the shoes of other people involved in the problem, including – where relevant – the manager. Another way of doing this is to present a similar problem but in a different context – a context in which the presenter can escape from his habitual way of judging business issues.

- Inconsistencies: the manager may spot inconsistencies in the material being explored; these might be between two remarks, or between what the presenter is saying and how he is behaving, or between two different behaviours. Checking these out may well reveal important elements in the problem.

- Significant omissions: what is not said may be just as revealing as what is said. Omissions may occur because the presenter really wishes to avoid the subject, or because awkwardness or embarrassment inhibit him. The manager must decide which (apparent) omissions he should challenge, and how he should set about doing so.

- Significant remarks: presenters may drop clues by making significant remarks without further explanation. They are usually hoping that the manager will pick up the clue and ask them about it; in this way they are 'obliged' to give information they would not like to be seen volunteering. This must be distinguished from the unconscious significant remark which the manager alone may spot as being important to the problem.

- Successive interviews: time constraints may make more than one interview necessary. There can be advantages in this: the interval may give the presenter an opportunity to re-think his position under more relaxed circumstances; and there may be specific homework – some investigation perhaps – which is needed before exploration can continue. The manager is advised to keep notes of previous interviews; these will remind him of what has happened, and help him to prepare for the next interview.

- Pencil and paper: it can be useful when much material is being explored to use a pencil and paper to record and summarize the position in a suitable diagram, built up by both participants. This bird's eye view may enable them to see the elements of the problem as a whole, and therefore more easily distinguish the key areas for attention or action.

- Practice.

8 Exploration –
the Synthesis

This is the final chapter on the Exploration stage. There is a brief reminder of the elements involved, with a diagram to permit them to be seen as a whole. Finding the core of the problem is essentially no different from any other methodical approach to problem solving: that is, it proceeds by way of forming hypotheses that appear to accord with the facts, and modifying these as the exploration continues until a working hypothesis which gives the best fit is agreed by the participants. Within this structure the particular skills and methods of solving problems face to face are employed. The process is completed by establishing who or what has to be changed if the problem is to be put right.

In Chapter 5 we looked at the purpose of the Exploration stage. Starting from the material presented during the Listening stage (and mutually understood by the participants) the task was to find the core of the problem, and to establish who or what had to change in order to put matters right. And this had to be done bearing in mind that the solution would be implemented through chosen goals. The setting of the goals would be the work of the Goal setting stage, but successful exploration would often indicate what those goals were likely to be. In Chapter 6 we looked at the six basic methods used for conducting exploration; and in Chapter 7 we looked at a number of skills which supplemented these methods.

Looking at the whole process

If you now turn to Figure 8.1, you will see the complete exploration process. The objective of finding the core of the problem is set centrally, and there is a reminder of the Goal setting stage which follows. Reading clockwise, you will first see a reminder of the general spirit in which good exploration should be conducted. Next appear the six basic methods, followed by a listing of the supplementary skills. Finally there is a box called HYPOTHESIS TESTING, and it is on this we shall be concentrating in this chapter.

Building a synthesis by means of hypotheses

The dictionary defines *synthesis* as 'the building up of separate conception, propositions or facts into a connected whole'. This is a process with which we are all familiar. For example, building a model aeroplane or furniture from a kit requires examining all the component parts, deciding what they contribute to the whole, discovering how they go together, and building them into the 'connected whole'. Because a kit is involved there is reason to believe that there is a connected whole into which they can be built (not always verified in my case) and there may be plans provided to assist this. Business situations are more open-ended – there may be no connected whole to find, or the connected whole eventually built may be the best of a number of unsatisfactory compromises. But the process is the same. For example, in the face of falling profits a large number of elements may have to be examined. Amongst them might be: cost of production, effectiveness of distribution, price mark-up, state of the market, appropriateness of products for the market, tax planning, etc. At the beginning of his investigation the manager might have no idea about the cause of the problem – although his general experience may tell him where he should look first and what sort of examination he should conduct. But, as the investigation continues, he will begin to form hypotheses as to the nature of the problem. He might, for instance, surmise, after looking at

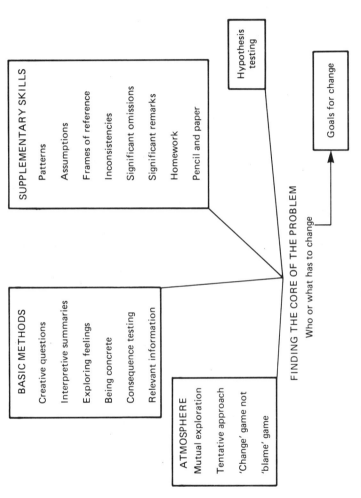

Figure 8.1   Summary of the Exploration stage

113

sales figures, that the key lies in motivating his distributors to achieve higher targets. But in the earlier stages he will not settle on this hypothesis until he has examined all the factors. Perhaps his review will show that the products are overpriced for the market; and then he must decide whether this comes from an overgenerous mark-up or high production costs. It is possible that he will consider several hypotheses before he is confident that he has chosen the best one. Having done so he has to consider what changes are necessary and what the consequences of implementing them may be. In this process he may see that there is more than one problem. For instance, the difficulty of selling high-priced goods may have demotivated his distribution, and he may need to address this in concert with lowering his production costs. He will also be discarding some potential elements as irrelevant – for example, tax planning may turn out to be efficient, and thus not contributing to the problem.

The problems which a manager may be called upon to solve face to face follow a closely parallel course. There is the special factor of the problem presenter (the manager is helping another person to solve the problem rather than doing it himself) and the complexity may vary from a five-minute problem of little consequence up to a problem of the complexity described above. Indeed, if a group managing director were to be discussing the profitability of a subsidiary with its chief executive the problem above might be the one being presented.

An example in action

When the Exploration stage begins neither manager nor presenter may have formed a hypothesis about the core of the problem. Consequently the best course is to start examining, through the methods I have described, the areas and aspects which a combination of experience and guesswork suggest may provide promising clues. And before long some kind of hypothesis will begin to form in the mind:

In the story of Margaret whose department has been showing low productivity (please refer to p. 86 in order to understand what follows), the manager elicits the reason that she has a number of staff away sick. At this stage the hypothesis in Margaret's mind is that this is the beginning and the end of the problem – given a week or two, the problem will correct itself. Her manager is not so sure and, in looking for a pattern, he discovers that her department has had a poor sickness record over a long period. At this stage he forms the hypothesis that the problem is not one of mere coincidence but has to do with how the department is managed.

Getting locked in

There is an immediate danger here. If the manager locks himself into this hypothesis he may find himself looking for – and inevitably finding – evidence to support this, and failing to notice evidence which runs counter to it. And he may well be clever enough in his questioning of Margaret to steer her into agreeing with this. (You may remember the story of secretary, Katy, who was talked into admitting that she was a disorganized person on the evidence of her untidy desk.) So, at this stage, his hypothesis must be very tentative – and his investigation of it very delicate:

He puts the pattern to her, and asks her to consider whether coincidence is an adequate explanation or whether there is some common factor which, if not corrected, will lead to the situation continuing. Margaret thinks about this, and agrees. Asked to suggest possible reasons, Margaret says she thinks it is that she has a high proportion of female staff, and that this inevitably means a poorer than average sickness record.

Testing Margaret's hypothesis

At this stage the manager has some confirmation that there is a common cause, but now Margaret has formed the new hypothesis that this is the poorer sickness record of female staff; she has not recognized the possibility of a management problem. The manager invites Margaret to test her idea:

He recognizes that Margaret is making an assumption about female staff which may or may not be true. When he tests this by asking for evidence Margaret says that 'everyone knows that women take more sick leave than men.' So they both study the company's sickness records – excluding Margaret's department – and she accepts that there is little difference between males and females; and certainly not enough to explain her situation. During their discussion of this point Margaret remarks that 'these young girls nowadays have no sense of responsibility – all they're interested in is their time off, there's no dedication to the job.'

Confronting Margaret, with tact

The manager now has a strong feeling that his original hypothesis was right. Margaret's attitude, as evidenced by this significant remark, is negative towards her staff. It looks as if she might be handling them badly with the result that they view her in much the same way as she apparently views them.

He feels the evidence is sufficiently strong to risk confronting her with this possibility, but – knowing this could be a sensitive matter – he does it with tactful question, by saying: 'I'm just wondering, Margaret, whether your view that young people have no sense of dedication has communicated itself to your staff. Could your people have picked up the idea that you don't expect too much of them? If so, it might affect their loyalty to you and the job. D'you think that's possible?' Margaret reddens at this, but she controls her feelings and thinks about the question. Then she says: 'No, I'm sure it's not that. I've always had young people in my department because I get most of the school leavers. So I've always tried to make it pleasant for them – as a first experience of work. Only the other day someone found out it was my wedding anniversary, and they bought me some flowers and a beautiful card. I don't think they'd have done that if they didn't think something of me.'

The hypothesis that clicks

And her manager has to agree that she has made a good point. While he doesn't need to abandon the poor management hypothesis, it now seems rather unlikely. But then he notices a possible further pattern – Margaret has reminded him that her staff tends to be school leavers. Is it possible, he wonders, that that could be the core of the problem?

> He discusses this with Margaret, and they decide that this is most likely to be the case. It seems possible that putting so many youngsters together, sharing a mutual experience of a first job, makes them into quite a powerful group in which taking time off for trivial health reasons has become habitual. And, after exhausting all the other possibilities, the two of them decide that they will act on this hypothesis – while being ready to revise it if it proves wrong or inadequate.

Reviewing the example

The process we have witnessed in this account is quite straightforward in its structure. A number of potentially relevant facts have been examined; some have been rejected as not pertinent, but gradually some have come together in a way that seems to fit; they make a picture – a connected whole – which Margaret and her manager recognize as being likely to be the core of the problem. The method has been one which is familiar in all organized approaches to problem solving: initial hypotheses have been formed, and then checked against the facts; this has led to hypotheses being modified or abandoned, and to new hypotheses being formed. Eventually the exploration of the facts has led to the establishment of a hypothesis which has a good fit with the facts, and since no better can be found, it is accepted – at least provisionally.

Who or what has to change?

The Exploration stage is not yet finished because no attempt has been made to establish who or what has to change. This aspect of exploration is discussed in Chapter 5. In Margaret's case she and her manager are able to decide this without difficulty. They decide that having a department largely made up of school leavers is a mistake, and that it should be leavened with more experienced people – whose presence will, in any event, give the young people a better introduction to working. Thus one thing which has to be changed is an element in the company's organization, and only the company can do that. And this will take time. So Margaret agrees that meanwhile she can put more concentration into helping her staff to understand how their work fits into the whole picture, and to see how much depends on their high productivity. She will also give thought to how she can vary some of the work to avoid boredom and develop a sense of responsibility. At this point they will need to decide on some specific goals; and we shall start examining the principles of goal setting in the next chapter.

The account of Margaret and her manager illustrates the structure within which the skills of the Exploration stage are used. The chapter summary will remind us of the basic points.

Summary

- The structure of the Exploration stage is built around the process of forming hypotheses which are initially very tentative, and open to revision.

- As the Exploration stage continues the relevant facts are established and examined. This may lead to the modification of early hypotheses, or to the formation of new ones. The participants are looking for the best fit of facts, and this forms the hypothesis on which they need to work.

- In order to elucidate the facts the manager is likely to need a number of the skills and methods explained in earlier chapters; and he must preserve the atmosphere of mutuality in which both participants are working as a team at the problem, and the object is to put the problem right – not to assign blame.

- The Exploration stage is not complete until who or what has to change in order to rectify the problem has been established.

9 Goal setting – the Principles

This chapter considers the Goal setting stage, and emphasizes its importance in turning the good intentions of the participants into effective action. The essential criteria for achievable goals are introduced (to be developed in the next chapter). The introduction and choice of goals are discussed, and their incorporation into the strategy most likely to bring about a solution. Chapter 11 looks at some further principles important in the setting of appropriate goals.

Good listening and good exploration require a range of skills, some of which do not come easily to individual managers, and most of which need continual practice in order to achieve excellence. And so it can be something of a relief to arrive at the Goal setting stage. As managers we are task-oriented, and the setting of goals for action brings us right back into a familiar and clearcut area. In fact it fits so well with our habitual activity that this is a section of the book to skim through, we know it well enough.

Not so, I fear. The LEGUP process operates as a whole: as with a chain the ultimate effectiveness will be no better than the weakest link. And the weakest link often turns out to be the establishment of goals; it is done badly because it looks easy, and it isn't; it is done badly because the methods look straightforward, and they aren't. And often it is done badly because it isn't done at all.

Our own experience of accomplishing goals

In order to see some of the difficulties encountered in goal setting it may help to consider the contrast between a good intention which is never properly realized, and an objective which is successfully accomplished. It may be that the road to hell is paved with good intentions; it is certainly true that the road to mediocrity is littered with the shards of what we once intended to do. If I admit that this is true of me, I do so in the confidence that I am not alone. The items, too many to list, are trivial: the occasion I resolved to keep my office tidy, the proper overhaul of my time control, the need to improve my business education, etc. – but, taken together, their accomplishment would have been a big improvement in my effectiveness as a business manager. Why did I not accomplish them? When the intention was formed I was eager and enthusiastic and the rewards of success were vivid in my imagination. But time passed, I was distracted by more immediate concerns, the burden of the task seemed to become heavier while the reward diminished and appeared more remote – in a matter of days or weeks the good intention had seeped out of my mind, and the matter lapsed.

Fortunately, and to my relief, I discovered that these failures were not the result of an inordinately weak will, or even incompetence. They were the result of ignorance of how people need to tackle their good intentions if they are to have a reasonable chance of achieving results. There is no magic formula because there will always be a tension between the desire to improve and the effort required, but there is a commonsense and realistic method of turning good intentions into practical goals which takes into account the inertia of human nature and maximizes the chance of success. However, our task in this book is not self-improvement but the solution of problems face to face. Therefore we will look at the method of goal setting in that context, although it may help to reflect on our own experience while doing so. If, incidentally, it helps anyone to improve their personal record of accomplishment, that is an uncovenanted dividend.

An overview of the method

The enemies of accomplishment can be listed under four main headings. The first is that we fail to define what it is exactly which needs to be accomplished. We have a vaguely expressed aspiration which is never made concrete enough to form a goal: we are firing in the general direction of the enemy, but there is no specific target in our sights.

The second is that we do not ensure that our intentions are realistic. It may be that we simply do not have the personal capacity to achieve the intention, or we may lack the skills or material resources to do so. Sometimes the step we want to take is too large, and when we face it we grow fainthearted. An important issue here is that the rewards to be gained are often in the future whereas the effort faces us immediately; and human beings respond badly when reward and effort do not come closely together. This issue is discussed separately in Chapter 11.

The third is that we do not define our intention in terms of observable behaviour. And since behaviour is the only hard evidence we have of change, there is no way of measuring success.

The fourth is that we do not always check that the intention is worthwhile. It may have sounded a good idea at the time, but is it really going to bring about a change or improvement that we value highly enough to go through the effort of bringing it to success?

These four points combine into a useful mnemonic:

> **C**oncrete
> **R**ealistic
> **O**bservable
> **W**orthwhile

which spell the word CROW – because an accomplished goal is something to CROW about. And it's useful to have such a checklist because it acts as a discipline at the Goal setting stage, enabling the satisfactoriness of possible goals to be quickly verified. In this chapter we shall look at entering into the Goal setting stage, and at some important general points which need to be observed. In the next, we

shall examine Concrete, Realistic, Observable and Worthwhile in more detail.

Starting goal setting

I have already suggested that the successful accomplishment
of the Exploration stage brings to the participants' minds the
sort of goals which might be needed to bring about the
desired changes. In Chapter 5 Roger was discussing his poor
sales results with his manager. The core of the problem
turned out to be weak closing techniques; this suggested that
the completion of additional training in this, followed by
achieving a target ratio of closes to sales interviews, might
form the appropriate goals. In the story of Drake, which
followed, the need to communicate to the accountant in his
own language suggested that a first goal might be to establish
with the accountant directly where the blockage lay.

But this may be dangerous because arriving at something
which sounds like an appropriate goal may lead the participants to assume that the Goal setting stage has already been
completed. It is better for the manager to regard the goals
which so naturally emerge from good exploration as no more
than a warning that the time for deliberate goal setting has
arrived, and to use them as a useful starting point for the
process. And he has the opportunity to make this explicit to
the problem presenter so that it becomes clear that this is
one problem where the solutions are going to be followed
through in a practical and definite way:

> 'Now that we've established, Roger, that the problem lies in your
> technique for closing sales, and that some extra training and
> some new targets might help here, let's try and work out some
> goals which will put matters right.

> 'So we're agreed, Drake, that you'll never get your new equip-
> ment budget through the accountant unless you can put it in a
> way which he'll understand. So let's look at some specific ways
> in which you might set about that.'

A choice of goals

In describing the Exploration stage I emphasized the importance of examining a number of hypotheses and trying to keep an open mind until the very best fit had been made. This was important because of the human tendency to grasp at the first credible explanation, and to cling on to it, as though laying it on one side for a moment would somehow allow it to slip away like quicksilver. Similarly there is a strong temptation to settle for the first goal which seems appropriate, and to follow that through without considering whether better alternatives can be found. Of course it will often happen that the first goal put forward still seems the best at the end of the examination; but no harm has been done by exposing oneself to the possibility of finding a better answer. For instance, sending Roger for training to improve his techniques for closing sales – so that he will achieve his targets – sounds a good idea, but there are other possibilities: he might make some joint calls with a salesman who is particularly good at closing sales, or he might undertake to note on his interview report sheet how many attempts he made to close at each occasion. Margaret, whose problem is the absentee rate of her young staff, is considering communicating to them their importance in the company's operations; but she might also think about the value of running a points competition for good attendance, or setting up little cooperative work teams which would create pressure from peers not to let the side down.

Selecting goals

A variety of options may also prove to be necessary because some of the possible goals may fail under one or more of the criteria of the CROW test. Let's just apply this in a brief way to Margaret's goal of putting 'more concentration into helping her staff to understand how their work fits into the whole picture and to see how much depends on their high productivity'.

- Is the goal *Concrete*? 'Putting more concentration' doesn't sound at all concrete. We have a vague idea of what is intended, but no more than that. How would we recognize when Margaret had succeeded? How much more is 'more'?

- Is the goal *Realistic*? It's hard to tell while it's so vague. But we should at least want to know whether Margaret had the personal resources – ability to communicate and so forth – and the sort of relationship with staff that would make this possible. We should also need to consider Margaret's capacity to persevere with her goal if it proves to be discouraging in the early stages. In addition, we would need to explore how ready the young staff might be to absorb the question of their importance to the company when their personal priorities are much more immediate and exciting.

- Is the goal *Observable*? How will Margaret judge that the lessons have gone home? This is going to be difficult when the goal is so vague; we don't know what level of understanding we are expecting from staff, whether it is emotional or intellectual understanding, and no immediate practical means of testing success suggests itself.

- Is the goal *Worthwhile*? It seems obvious that a greater sense of their worth to the company will motivate the staff to better attendance. But whether this would be true or not needs to be considered. Do young staff react well to this? Might it not make them feel a greater security in their occasional absences since the company can't do without them? Might it simply not connect in their minds, and lead to no real improvement?

This is not in any way to condemn the objective out of hand. It could well be that by thinking it through and expressing it more clearly a satisfactory goal could be formulated. But it is certainly possible that under examination the goal would turn out to be lacking in some vital respect; or that a better goal, or supplementary goals, would be needed.

A strategy for goal setting

In order to avoid confusion it is necessary for me to distinguish between goals and sub-goals. In the case of Roger, the goal would be to improve his sales results. It should, of course, conform to the CROW criteria; thus, in order to make it concrete, Roger and his manager might agree to 'an increase of 25 per cent in sales revenue within 6 months'. Both of them would then know whether Roger had succeeded. But, during the Exploration stage, they discovered that the root cause of the problem was his poor performance at turning sales calls into completed sales. This suggests that there should be an intermediate goal which will be a probable means of achieving the ultimate goal (improving his ratio of closes to sales interviews); this is called a sub-goal. But in order to achieve this sub-goal Roger will have to do other things; one suggestion was that he should have training in closing techniques. To be consistent we should call this a sub-sub-goal, since it leads to a sub-goal – which leads to the goal. But for simplicity I shall use the term 'goal' to cover all of these, and only specify sub-goals when the context needs it.

Consequently we are rarely speaking of one goal in the solution of a problem. It is usually necessary to have a sort of hierarchy of goals and sub-goals to achieve success. Strategy may sound too grand a word, but it is appropriate. Just as a commander-in-chief may have a network of objectives (sub-goals) to win the war (goal), so may a problem solver. Both he and the commander-in-chief would be wise to plan in advance. So Drake, who wants a budget for his new computer equipment to be agreed by an old fashioned accountant, knows what his goal is. But his strategy comprises discovering where the accountant's difficulties lie, bringing the accountant nearer to his side by demonstrating that he appreciates his problems, and preparing his submission in a form which meets the accountant's criteria. And these form his sub-goals.

You may have noticed that the sub-goals do not necessarily or inevitably bring about the goal itself – any more than capturing this town or securing that beachhead will certainly win the war. Thus Drake may complete all his sub-goals and still be met with a blank refusal, or Margaret may make all her staff enthusiastic about their role in the company and not improve the attendance record. They can never be more than what appears to be the most satisfactory means likely to bring about the goal. Therefore flexibility, and readiness to revise the strategy, are required.

> Benedict has found that he is way behind with his administration; following the earlier stages of the problem solving process he establishes that his goal is to clear his in-tray each day, and to do so in less than an hour. He examines a number of possible sub goals: asking his secretary to weed out some items to deal with herself; tackling his in-tray at a predetermined time, refusing all interruptions; delegating a higher proportion of items to staff; taking a speed-reading course; selecting a small number of trade magazines to review instead of trying to see them all; dictating to a pocket recorder rather than to his secretary. He decides that the first and last sub-goals are the best ones on which to concentrate – at least initially. These give him further sub-goals: training his secretary in the items she can handle; obtaining the appropriate dictating machinery and, with his secretary, learning how to use it.

Benedict's strategy is shown in Figure 9.1. Such a diagram can often be helpful in deciding on a goal strategy, and provides a further example of how paper and pencil can help the problem solving manager.

Order and timing

Missing from Benedict's strategy are ordering and timing. No goal strategy can be considered complete until these have been established. The order in which sub-goals are tackled may be critical, and goals are rarely measurable unless a time by when they should be reached has been agreed. Timing can often be important in strategy, as Napoleon discovered when his army arrived in a deserted Moscow just in time for the Russian winter. In Benedict's case the ordering is implicit – the bottom sub-goals must be

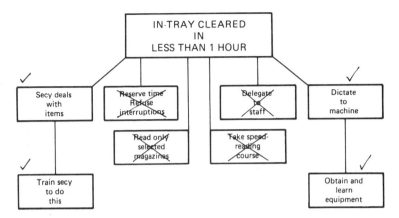

Figure 9.1   Benedict's good strategy

tackled first, and not much thought is needed to see that the equipment should be obtained before practising with it. But he will need a timetable for his sub-sub-goals and his sub-goals before he can set a target time for reaching his goal.

Summary

- Goal setting is the stage which converts an understanding of the problem into action which will solve it.

- While managers welcome it because it is action-centred, they sometimes assume that it needs no particular care – or even that it can look after itself.

- In order to give goals a chance of real success they need to satisfy the CROW criteria: Concrete, Realistic, Observable, Worthwhile.

- Goal setting should be introduced as a deliberate stage in the process so that both manager and presenter are working at the task in an orderly and discriminating way.

- There is a temptation to stick with the first credible goal which presents itself, but problem solvers need to look at a variety of possible goals in order to improve the chances of finding the best ones.

- Usually a hierarchy of goals is needed: there is a primary goal, which provides the solution to the problem; and sub-goals which are judged to be the most likely means of bringing about the primary goal. These sub-goals may also have their own sub-goals needed for their achievement. A good goal setting strategy is crucial for the solution of many problems. A pencil and paper diagram may be helpful.

- The strategy should be completed by agreeing the timing and ordering of the goals and sub-goals.

10 Choosing Goals that Work

In this chapter the CROW criteria – Concrete, Realistic, Observable and Worthwhile – are examined against a number of examples. If the goals selected are going to have the very best chance of being achieved they will satisfy these criteria. If they do not they should be either modified or changed.

A working example

In order to provide a basis for examining CROW in action I will outline a background problem which can be used – together with other examples, when required – to illustrate the main points of goal setting.

> Helen is manager of your market intelligence department, and she is very frustrated. From time to time she submits reports to senior management which are based on careful research and long thought. Typically she will be recommending a course of action which she is confident the company should take in order to improve marketing success and therefore profitability. But few of her recommendations are ever accepted, and when she finally manages to discuss the report with her seniors (who appear to have little enough time to spare for this) it seems to her that the reports have been read only scantily or not at all. Since producing such reports is very much the heart of her job, she feels that she is able to contribute little of value, and has problems in motivating both herself and her team.

During the Listening stage Helen becomes quite emotional. She is angry with the company for asking her to do a job and then not making use of it. She believes that the company is really not prepared to make any marketing changes, and her function only exists so that the directors can pretend to themselves that they are up to date and adventurous. She suspects that at least one of the key directors resents her because she is a woman. Helen is confident in the quality of her work, and when she describes the substance of some of her most recent reports you are impressed. If some of her reports were not accepted she would understand, but when all, or nearly all, are rejected she feels she has every reason to believe that someone up there doesn't like her.

After investigating a number of points in the Exploration stage you arrange for another meeting with her the following week. Meanwhile you ask her to let you have two or three of her recent reports - the ones of which she is particularly proud. When she does so you immediately regret having volunteered: each report is a massive volume! There are reams of statistics and a multitude of appendices. Each point is discussed meticulously, with every detail covered. You have to read several sections many times over before you are clear what she is recommending. And, from time to time, she employs a critical style which suggests that if the management does not take up her suggestions it is are failing to give proper leadership. Your concern for Helen sustains you as you read right through one report, but nothing will induce you to do more than flip through the others to confirm that they are similar.

When you next meet Helen you work at changing her frame of reference. You put her into the mind of a busy director, and ask her to imagine possible reactions to such a report. At first she has difficulty in making the leap, but gradually she begins to see that, in trying too hard to please, she has ensured failure. Even she, she finally admits, would be rather unenthusiastic about studying such a report. You both agree that this does not prove that she is not the victim of the directors' stupidity or prejudice, but that this cannot really be tested until she has submitted more readable reports. And so, as you move into the Goal setting stage you are both agreeing that improving the presentation of her reports is the place to start.

Concrete goals

Both you and Helen have an idea about what 'improving the presentation of the reports' means. Or have you? After all, before your discussion began Helen genuinely believed that the reports were excellent, and it was this which fuelled her anger when they were ignored. But, in the light of Helen's new insight into the needs of her readers she may be able to see that this will not do as her ultimate goal. Superbly presented reports will achieve nothing unless the readers react in the right way. So she might rephrase her goal in her readers' terms, perhaps: 'present reports in such a way that the directors like them'. But this is not very concrete; what does 'like them' mean? So it may help to try and define how the directors would behave if they did like the reports. After some consideration Helen suggests that if they liked them they would read them, and would perhaps want to discuss them with her. This looks more satisfactory, but then Helen realizes that this won't solve her problem altogether – to do that her reports must be acted on. Being realistic she accepts that this will not always happen, but she thinks it would be reasonable to expect that at least one in three would lead to action substantially in line with her recommendations. At this point you discuss timescale with her. You may want to revise this later but for now you both think that the goal should be in two parts: the first will start to be accomplished from the presentation of her next report; if it is presented in the right way it will be read and discussed. The second goal cannot be properly tested in the short term; she will have had to submit a number of reports before it will be fair to judge whether one in three is being acted upon. At the end of this discussion the goal begins to look like this:

1   To present reports in such an attractive way that the reader either invites Helen to discuss them, or agrees readily to a discussion. Such discussion should show by the quality of his review that the director has studied and absorbed the material. Success to be initially judged following her next report scheduled for September, and confirmed by reaction to subsequent reports.

   2   Further, to present reports of such value that in, on average, one out of three occasions positive action in line with the report is taken by the company. Success to be monitored after three reports have been submitted, and judged after six reports.

From 'improving the quality of the reports', which means nothing very definite, to the quite clear definition of goals above is an important step. Now Helen knows what she has to do in order to succeed, and her knowledge is concrete.

Concrete sub-goals

She has not yet decided how she is going to achieve this goal, and so you and she must discuss the possible sub-goals which will lead to this outcome. For the purpose of studying concreteness we will take just one possible sub-goal and examine it.

You both agree that it is going to be important to grab the reader's attention right at the beginning – before the report gets put on a shelf. But merely to have a sub-goal which says 'this report must grab the reader's attention' fails the concreteness test straight away. However, the Exploration stage has shown that the first problem is the forbidding bulk of the reports. Helen considers whether it would be possible to prune the reports of all information not strictly relevant to their purpose. She thinks that this might be done, but that it would only shorten the average report by about twenty per cent. Helpful, but not sufficient. As you both discuss further other suggestions emerge – summarizing the key statistics in the report itself and relegating the detailed figures to a separately bound appendix, for instance. When this work is finished you have agreed about a number of concrete steps which will support the sub-goal of reducing the forbidding bulk of the report; and this, in turn, will support the goal of inducing the recipient to read it. Other sub goals will, of course, be necessary, and these would be developed in the same fashion, always looking for the concrete action which will achieve the desired result.

Intangible goals

Although helping Helen to present acceptable reports is a very demanding task it does have the advantage that it can be turned quite easily into concrete goals. But some problems are more intangible, and it is often hard to find a way of expressing them concretely:

> 'I want to get on better with my colleagues. I want them to like me.'

You may like to think for a moment about how that would be expressed in concrete terms.

A good way to approach this is to ask the question: how would one know that the objective had been achieved? This obliges the mind to think in terms of the sort of behaviour which would indicate success. After all, the presenter in such a case has only been able to judge that he is not liked through his colleagues' behaviour. He may well, in the earlier stages, have used phrases like 'I just get the feeling that I'm unpopular'. But the Exploration stage should have revealed that his feeling – if it is not imaginary – is based on behavioural evidence: for instance, colleagues may habitually choose not to sit with him in the works canteen. This can simply be reversed to decide the behaviour which would indicate liking. Thus the objective might be:

> 'I shall know my colleagues are beginning to like me when they respond to my greeting in the morning, when they draw me into social discussion, and when they choose to join me in the works canteen.'

Concreteness as a business discipline

Making objectives concrete is a generally desirable characteristic in business. And it is often avoided – with the result that much of business meanders its way in the general direction of the sea, often taking the longest route and only arriving at its destination by little more than chance. One reason for this is understandable, if hardly excusable. Define an objective, and you have yourself on a hook. Leave it decently vague, and neither you nor anyone else knows if you have succeeded or failed. Some skilled vagueness operators form their objectives by hindsight: if an enterprise turns out well they subtly discover that this was their objective after all; if it turns out badly there is nothing sufficiently definite by which their failure can be judged. Fortunately problem solving is less susceptible to this temptation since the presenter is motivated to put matters right, and to know that he has done so. However, the second temptation is present in problem solving just as it is elsewhere. This is the old temptation to avoid hard thinking. Making an objective concrete requires you to consider what you really want or need to do. It brings your intention out into the open where it can be examined and judged. In the glare of this light objectives which sounded so good in their vague formulation often begin to look unreasonable, or unrealistic, or even not what you intended at all.

Exercises in concreteness

Here are some examples of vaguely expressed intentions. Using your imagination to fill in the circumstances, try to make them concrete. Remember to use the question: how would I know that this goal had been completed?

1 'I want to be more open in expressing my opinions at meetings. When I disagree with the general view I want to have the courage to say so.'

2 'So often by the end of the day I realize I have been very busy doing routine things, and the important things have been left to one side. I want to correct this.'

3 'I'm going to need a higher quality staff than I have at present if I'm going to take on these new responsibilities.'

4 'I'm making too many mistakes in my calculations. I've got to be more accurate with my arithmetic.'

5 'I just don't feel motivated any more; every day seems a
   drag. How can I become enthusiastic so that I do my work
   better?'

Realistic goals

It is encouraging that so many problem presenters reach the
Goal setting stage enthusiastic about putting matters to
rights. Having expressed and explored in a constructive way
a problem which may have been nagging at them for some
time, they are now over-eager to accomplish at once all the
sub-goals which will ensure success. The manager may well
feel reluctant to counsel patience, yet this may be the correct
course.

This can come about because the goals they choose may
be too ambitious. Helen may want every report to be read
by every director, and to be acted on in every respect.
Margaret may want to breed a pentecostal enthusiasm for
the company's interests among her staff so that no one goes
absent for illness except to die. So the manager must gently
bring them down to earth and help them to establish objectives which are within the bounds of reasonable possibility.
Besides the obvious reason for this, there is another one to
which I have already referred: the susceptibility we all share
to discouragement. It is sometimes said that the higher you
aim the higher you are likely to get – even if you never
achieve your target. But this ignores the fact that continually
missing a target is to be continuously deprived of the satisfaction of successful achievement. Donkeys may be mentally
equipped to follow all day a carrot suspended in front of
their noses; human beings are not.

Splitting the goal

A goal may not be unreasonably ambitious, and yet it may
not be unrealistic to achieve it in one step. It is not over-
ambitious for me to wish to go to the upper floor of my
house, but I have the choice of taking a flying leap or using
the stairs. Helen may be quite reasonable in expecting that

all, or nearly all, of her reports should be read and grasped by the recipients, but she might be wiser to accept that, in the early stages, this won't happen – perhaps she will have to experiment with her changes in presentation before she gets them right, or perhaps it will take time before the recipients realize that her reports have become readable. Unless her strategy takes this into account she may be back to you next month saying that she's getting nowhere and now despairs of success. Let's imagine her manager proposing an additional sub-goal (step on the stair) to help with this:

> 'Here's an idea to think about, Helen. You've said that you get on quite well with Mr Briggs. When you've prepared your next report taking all the changes into account, why don't you go to see him with it before you circulate it generally? If you tell him that you're working on making reports more readable, and ask him to tell you if he thinks you've succeeded or where you could improve further, you'll kill two birds with one stone. You'll get some useful criticism, and the word will soon spread in the directors' dining room that the reports are attractive to read.

Narrow the concentration

As dangerous as creating too remote an objective is trying to do too many things at once. You may remember from the last chapter how Benedict developed some possible sub-goals for reducing the amount of time he spent dealing with his in-tray. There were six of these (see p. 126), from which he eventually selected two. Imagine if he had attempted to tackle all six at the same time. Each of the sub-goals was useful in itself but, taken together, the result would be confusion, and nothing would be properly done. So it is important to focus attention on a small number of goals at a time. It may even be wise to take them one by one. This approach was described in the first chapter when I suggested that the Benjamin Franklin self-organizer could provide a useful method for tackling the skills of LEGUP in a concentrated way. The self-organizer can be useful to the problem presenter too, as this example shows:

By the end of his annual assessment Victor has accumulated quite a list of desirable changes: better time control, improved delegation to his subordinates, better understanding of company budgets, better control of promotional reports. He is anxious to get on with all of these, but his boss counsels patience. He reminds him of Benjamin Franklin's thirteen-week self-organizer. He tells him how Franklin identified thirteen virtues in which he wanted to improve but, instead of advancing on all fronts, he allocated a week to each virtue. During that week he would concentrate on that virtue – surrounding himself with appropriate reminders. He would take the next virtue on his list for the following week. Meanwhile he left the remaining twelve to their ordinary chance, knowing that four times a year they would receive his concentration. He helps Victor to draw up a schedule in this spirit so that he concentrates on each of the improvements in turn, leaving the others to their ordinary chance. Victor will report his progress at the end of each cycle.

Tackling goals in the best order

When a goal is dependent on the completion of a sub-goal the order decides itself. But sometimes there is a choice. There are no firm rules for this but it is advisable to start, wherever possible, with an objective which can be reasonably easily accomplished, and which will make a significant difference. If Helen has two sub-goals – shortening her reports and providing a sharp two-page executive summary with a list of recommendations to preface the report – she might well choose to start with the latter. It will take less time to accomplish, and provide her with tangible evidence of succeeding with a goal. People who have wrestled with a problem for some time often lack confidence that they can really deal with it. An early success gives them the encouragement they need to persevere with the rest. And, surprisingly often, the achievement of one goal has a strong bearing on the achievement of others:

Helen returns a few days later bearing a crisp two-page summary of her last report, feeling very proud of it. She then says that the process of extracting the summary demonstrated to her how the report lacked structure. Now, she says, she can re-order the report to give it much more clarity, and she will have a better idea of what she can omit in order to shorten it.

Denzil has a very introverted member of staff whom he wants to bring out and help to become a useful member of the group. He decides on an initial, very modest, objective: to talk with him for a few minutes every day on football scores, in which he is known to have an interest. Later Denzil reports that after a few of these chats the staff member changed the subject, and began to talk about business matters. Denzil now has a second problem: how to stop him talking now the dam gates have been unblocked.

Goals that fail

Much of what I have had to say under the CROW criterion of Realistic has been concerned with perseverance. Unless goals are realistic for the presenter they will be too difficult to achieve, and discouragement will set in. Sometimes goals fail because they turn out, with hindsight, to have been wrongly chosen – experience proves that they are not work-able, or that they do not achieve their intended result. However, the damage can be limited by warning the presenter of the possibility, and by reminding him that at the Pursuit stage the goals will be reviewed and, if necessary, revised.

Presenters that fail

Another problem is encountered more frequently: the presenter undertakes a realistic goal, and fails at it. Thus Denzil might have attempted his chats with his silent staff member, and met a completely blank result. Very discour-aging. Here, also, it helps to warn the presenter of this possibility; it is important that he should consider what he might do if things go wrong:

'Denzil, these chats about football scores sound just the thing to get some conversation going. But suppose this fellow just simply doesn't respond. Maybe he just grunts at you, or perhaps he accepts a little conversation but won't take it any further. What will you do then?'

'Helen, let's suppose Mr Briggs agrees to read through your report and to let you have his criticism. Then you hear nothing. And perhaps, a week later, you're in his office for something else – and there's the report lying where he put it, untouched. We don't think that's likely to happen, but it could, couldn't it? How would you feel about that?'

In this way the presenter is prepared emotionally for initial failure, so that he is less likely to be thrown by it; he is also able to formulate contingency plans to deal with it.

Realistic for whom?

A further reason why a realistic goal may still result in failure and discouragement is because the presenter lacks the ability or skills to carry it out. Margaret may want her staff to see the important part they play in company success but perhaps she is a poor communicator; or maybe her irritation with the staff now makes it difficult for them to be willing to listen. Helen may wish to provide a sharp two-page summary for her reports but lacks the skill to extract the basics from the mass of details, and is unable to do it. The goals were fine – for someone else, but not for Margaret or Helen. It may therefore help to construct a 'pushmepull-you' chart. This is a simple device for analysing the factors which are likely to help the accomplishment of a goal, and those which are likely to hinder it. Once completed it not only identifies the likely course of events it also indicates where action might usefully be taken to improve the balance. In order to study it in action we will take the case of Walter, who wants to achieve better delegation to his staff so that he has more time for his own specialist duties. We will leave this objective in its current vague form since we do not need to refine it further in order to demonstrate the chart in action.

A blank pushmepullyou chart is shown in Figure 10.1.

Figure 10.1   A blank pushmepullyou chart

You will see that a reminder of the objective forms the centre line of the chart. Above, with an arrow pointing to the right, is a space in which to write all the factors which will help to achieve the objective. Below, with the arrow to the left, should be written all the hindering factors. Although I have introduced the pushmepullyou chart at this point, it is valuable at many of the problem solving stages, and can be easily adapted to fit a precise purpose. The conversation with Walter continues:

Looking at the blank chart Walter, like most of us, can see the difficulties more readily than the facilities. 'The first problem is that delegation takes time; often I'd find it less trouble to do the job myself.' But after a few moments' thought he says: 'Still I suppose that can't really be right. If I did everything myself I wouldn't really need any staff. So maybe one good thing about delegation is that we get a better workload covered.' When he reviews his skills he decides that he's not very patient, but expects his staff to understand what he has in mind without him having to spell it out. Then he is irritated if the result isn't to his liking. But he recognizes that he really wants his staff to do well – he feels great satisfaction if a delegated task really comes off. 'Of course I do worry while the work's being done and I like to go and have a look at it from time to time – and I know that makes my people nervous,' he says. But he claims that that's not altogther his fault: 'You know what a perfectionist Mr Simkins is. I've learnt how to do things the way he likes them, and I can't really expect my staff to get that right unless I keep pretty close behind them.'

Figure 10.2   Half-completed pushmepullyou chart

Walter would no doubt think of many further items, but let's try and catch what he has said so far on the chart. See Figure 10.2.

Even at this stage Walter and his manager are able to pick out factors which need some work. Is Walter yet convinced that the long term advantages of good delegation outweigh the short term nuisance and delays of getting it started? If his motivation is not there, he can expect problems. Then, how about his communication skills? He appears to be having difficulty in getting his requirements across to his staff – perhaps he is not using his imagination to see how his briefing looks from the recipient's point of view. But his wish to have his staff do well, and the satisfaction he derives when a delegated job comes off will undoubtedly help. Then there's an outside factor – Mr Simkins. Is Walter right in supposing that he's only happy with work done in a particular way? If so, can Mr Simkins be persuaded to live with a greater variety of approaches? Or is it possible to teach the staff some do's and don'ts which will at least ameliorate the problem?

By the time the pushmepullyou chart is completed Walter and his boss will have a good idea of whether the goal is a realistic one for Walter. Perhaps some sub-goals will be needed. And he may require training or other kinds of support if he is to succeed. We will return to this last point in looking at the Underpinning stage.

You may like to practise developing a pushmepullyou chart of your own. To do this you will need to pick a particular goal which you think you might want to achieve – leaving work at a more reasonable hour in the evening perhaps, or improving your time control. Draw the chart and fill in the factors in your circumstances (as broad as you like) which help or hinder this goal. Then consider how you would set about reinforcing the helps, or capitalizing on them; and follow this by seeing how you might reduce the hindrances, or their impact.

Observable goals

In looking at the process of turning a goal from being a vague wish into a concrete action I suggested that a good question would be: how would I know if this goal had been accomplished? Here I was borrowing from the criterion of observability. Unless a goal has implicit in it some way in which its success can be measured it is impossible to tell whether it has been accomplished. And two penalties can be paid for this: first, the satisfaction of achieving the goal is denied; second, if the success of a second goal depends on the completion of the first, then we need to know that it has been completed. Therefore, although we shall have gone at least some way towards making a goal measurable through making it concrete, it cannot finally pass the scrutiny of manager and presenter unless its method of measurement has been made explicit, and both are clear that it is this measurement which will be used to judge its success.

Some organizations suffer from the 'experimental syndrome' whose motto is: 'If at first you don't succeed, make sure you never find out'. The syndrome comes into action when a company is faced by a decision about which it feels nervous. Rather than committing itself to a course of action, it labels it 'experimental'; and then undertakes it – feeling quite comfortable because no firm decision has been made. This sounds, at first sight, to be a very sensible way of proceeding. After all every activity should be reviewed periodically, and then confirmed or abandoned. The clue to the 'experimental syndrome' is that no criteria are established by which success or failure will be judged – and, often, no review period is set. Thus the experiment can continue for several years, or even until the oldest inhabitant who can remember its commencement has long retired. Problem solving is subject to the same temptation. Making a goal concrete is only the first stage, but being explicit about its measurement and the period after which its success will be judged is a necessary second stage.

> 'Margaret, we'll have solved this problem if the attendance rate of your department improves. What would you say was a reasonable level; should it be as high as the average for the whole company, or perhaps a lower rate because of the youth of your staff? And while we're about it, perhaps we ought to agree about when we would expect to see the improvements. Maybe we should have an early review to judge progress – and then another six months later to see if you have achieved your goal.'

> 'Helen, you're going to work on this last report of yours, and try to reduce its bulk before you present it. Let's agree a target for you; could you reduce it by half – or is that too ambitious?'

Making goal achievement observable – an exercise

Naturally we shall encounter the problem of measuring in some definite way a goal which resists being quantified. We shall not always succeed but it is necessary to make a goal as measurable as possible, and to resist the temptation to forget about measurement when it proves hard to set out in a convenient form. The difficulty will often turn out not to lie with the nature of the goal but with our laziness which persuades us that the task is too difficult.

On p. 134 I asked you to undertake a little exercise in making vague goals concrete. If you dodged the exercise, go back and have another look. If you did it successfully then you may want to compare your answers with the ones I suggest below. Mine are not 'correct' answers – because it depends on the circumstances – but they should indicate how choosing a way of measuring results gives an extra dimension of reinforcement. In fact, concreteness and observability make reinforced concrete – which ensures that goals are firmly set.

1   Vague goal: 'I want to be more open in expressing my opinions at meetings. When I disagree with the general view I want to have the courage to say so.'

   Observable goal: 'Starting on Monday I'll make a cross on my pad every time I hear something at a meeting with which I would like to disagree. If I do express disagreement I'll put a tick by the cross. At the end of the week I'll reckon up. If at least a third of the crosses are ticked, I'll know I've succeeded.'

2   Vague goal: 'So often by the end of the day I realize I've been very busy doing routine things, and the important things have been left to one side. I want to correct this.'

   Observable goal: 'Every evening before I leave work I'm going to make a note of three important things I plan to do the next day. They'll be my priorities – before I look at any routine work. The following evening I'll check. If I've got two of them done I've had a successful day. And I'm aiming to have three successful days out of five.'

3   Vague goal: 'I'm going to need a higher quality staff than I've got at present if I'm going to take on these new responsibilities.'

   Observable goal: 'I've made out a list of the posts I need to fill, and beside them I've put a list of minimum qualifications and a list of desirable additional qualifications. I shall succeed if all my new people pass the minimum test – provided they all have at least one of the desirable qualifications.'

4   Vague goal: 'I'm making too many mistakes in my calculations. I've got to be more accurate with my arithmetic.'

   Observable goal: 'Fred has agreed to check my addition on the bills for the next fortnight. He'll throw back at me any bill that's wrong. My objective is to get no more than one in ten back during the first week, and one in twenty back in the second week.'

5   Vague goal: 'I just don't feel motivated any more; every day seems a drag. How can I become enthusiastic so that I do my work better?'

Observable goal: 'I guess I'll know I'm over the hump when I'm no longer waking up on weekday mornings feeling depressed because it's a workday. Well, every day except Mondays. I don't want to ask the impossible.'

But don't get obsessed with measurement. In answering that exercise I deliberately chose rather precise and quantifiable measurements in order to demonstrate that it can be done. Use quantifiable measurements as often as possible, but – if they are quite inappropriate – be content if you and the presenter have some definite and objective way in which success can be judged.

Worthwhile goals

It may seem unnecessary to add that goals should be worthwhile. If it's not worthwhile it's not worth doing. But it's surprisingly easy to end up with goals which are really not going to achieve anything very much – or are not going to achieve what is intended.

For instance, look at goal 4, above, which is aimed at helping someone to improve the accuracy of their arithmetic. We don't know the full circumstances, but it's possible that a great deal of time could be saved by providing a calculating machine. Or perhaps there should be a routine which ensures that every addition is checked by someone. The work which is needed to achieve even a quite simple goal can be considerable, and energy is best saved for those which are worthwhile.

Goal 3, which concerns the recruitment of higher quality staff, reminds me of an occasion when I was recruiting for a new operation. It was very challenging, and I started with a determination only to use the very best people. But on reflection I realized that a number of jobs were really quite pedestrian, and only needed average staff to perform them. Indeed highly qualified staff would soon have been itching for more stimulating work – they would lose their concentration and probably be less reliable than the others. I changed my goal.

It is possible to be dazzled by the problem solving process so that it begins to become an end in itself. It is useful just before finally accepting a goal or a sub-goal to ask: is this really worthwhile? An ounce of commonsense at this stage (or at any stage) is worth a pound of theory.

Forward from here

When the goal strategy has been agreed, and the goals conform to the CROW criteria, there are two last jobs to be done. The first is to agree on the underpinning required for the achievement of the goals. This need may have been revealed by the pushmepullyou chart, and it will be discussed further in Chapter 12. The second is to arrange for follow up occasions or meetings to monitor or judge goals. This is covered in Chapter 13.

But, before leaving the subject of goal setting it is valuable to look a little more deeply into motivation. The professional students of behaviour teach that beyond the commonsense principles, like those of CROW, there are other principles – not so obvious to the ordinary observer – which have a bearing on the achievement of goals. The next chapter looks at these.

Summary

- No matter what care has been taken to select a variety of goals and sub-goals to solve the problem, it is necessary to subject them to the CROW criteria. If they cannot pass the tests they must either be modified so that they do, or changed for more satisfactory ones.

- Concreteness means working to express a goal so that both manager and presenter know quite clearly the nature of the goal; both know what is expected of the presenter, and both will be able to judge whether, and by when, it has been achieved.

- Realistic means choosing a goal where there is a reasonable practical expectation of accomplishment. Sometimes presenters, in their enthusiasm, select goals which are too ambitious; sometimes the goal is ultimately realistic but can only be achieved through steps, or sub-goals. Beware of too many goals at once; it is often better to concentrate on one or two at a time, and then add in others later. When several goals are identified the order in which they are undertaken may be important; where this is not dictated by the nature of the problem, the first goal should be reasonably easy and yet accomplish something in which the presenter can take pride. Presenters should be ready for possible failures, either because the goal was wrongly chosen or simply because it doesn't work; they should be asked to prepare for this possibility by forming contingency plans.

  A goal may be realistic in itself but not realistic for the presenter – because he lacks the capacity or the resources to carry it out. It may be useful to employ a pushmepullyou chart to analyse the helps and the hindrances. This may lead either to providing the additional help required, or to modifying the goal strategy to take the analysis into account.

- Observable means that goals should be expressed in a form which allows their success to be measured. Without this there will be no final way of judging success, and there will be reduced satisfaction from this lack of result. While some goals are easier to measure than others, some hard thinking will usually establish a reasonably satisfactory way – and one that is certainly better than nothing.

- Worthwhile means that, before a goal is finally accepted, it should be checked through the judgement of commonsense to make sure that it will have a good chance of achieving what is intended – and that what is intended is worth achieving.

11   Goals and Rewards

This, final, chapter of the Goal setting stage reviews the way in which people characteristically behave in order to maximize the benefits they receive. The examples we use help to define the nature of rewards and how they are perceived, which is directly relevant to the formulation of goals which have a good chance of being accomplished. It can also be useful at the Exploration stage to understand how rewards affect behaviour.

In the last two chapters we looked at methods of tackling the Goal setting stage which would help to ensure that the goals and sub-goals chosen would have the best chance of being executed. Lying behind these approaches, and implicit in many of them, was a basic principle which is so important in the problem solving process that it deserves a chapter to itself.

Expressed very simply the principle is: people behave according to the balance of benefits which they believe will be the outcome of their actions.

In so far as this principle is true, it follows that if the completion of goals provides more benefit on balance than not completing them they will be completed. And the reverse also follows.

I have expressed the principle in a bald way. And an immediate reaction may be to resist strongly the idea that human beings only follow what seems to be their best interests. After all, history is full of heroes and saints, and most of us can – I hope – think of instances in our own lives when we have acted selflessly. Yes, there are, thank God (literally), plenty of exceptions. But they remain exceptions, and we are concerned with the general rules on which we need to rely for the majority of our management activities. Let's start by looking at some examples:

> Jennifer is a sales promotion executive. She gives a great deal of thought and care to every promotion she undertakes, and on a number of occasions the quality of her work has brought her public approbation both within and outside the company. But there is a problem: her promotions are much too infrequent, and take several months to prepare. As a result the sales team do not have the constant and continual support they need in order to be successful. When the sales director analyses the situation he discovers that Jennifer finds the approbation she gets for a first-class job very rewarding. But running a programme of promotions is much less rewarding: to do this she has to delegate a great deal of the work and this lessens her personal involvement; the standard of each promotion will inevitably drop as their frequency increases; and there will be less kudos in running a general, continuous programme than there is in her coups – which have a much more dramatic effect.

Jennifer's behaviour appears illogical. She is quite intelligent enough to realize that a continuous programme is necessary for full success; indeed her job description makes it perfectly clear that she is responsible for the overall effectiveness of sales promotion, and she can see that she is falling down on this primary task. In order to understand what is happening we need to notice first that the reward of approbation she is receiving is not financial (it may turn out to be the reverse of financial if she gets the sack!); second, that the reward is immediate; and third, that the reward she believes she would get for doing a good overall job is long term (perhaps eventual promotion or a rise) and, in any event, may not be very exciting. Quite simply, Jennifer is getting a better balance of rewards from her current behaviour than she feels she would achieve by changing it.

Before we look at the principles behind this, let's take another example:

> Hamish suffers from a very busy boss. Whenever he asks for some time to discuss aspects of his work he is greeted by a gruff and irritated response. On the occasions when he has persisted and actually obtained his boss's attention, things are quite different. His boss listens carefully, and devotes as much care as is needed to Hamish's query. But, as time goes on, Hamish asks to see his boss less and less – it just seems too much hassle. One day Hamish makes a bad decision on a matter about which he should have consulted his boss. In taking him to task, the boss points out that he has always given Hamish the time and attention he has needed, and he cannot understand why he was not consulted.

There are similarities between Jennifer and Hamish. In both cases behaving differently would have served them better in the long run. But in the short term the advantage lay in continuing their current behaviour. Jennifer gets the reward of her sales promotion coups, Hamish avoids the unpleasantness of the struggle to see his boss.

But this balance of benefits need not apply just at the level of individuals; it can apply to a whole business, as this example shows:

> Stroniron Limited is a long-established engineering firm which built its reputation earlier this century by the high quality of its work. A small museum is kept in which the finest examples produced over the years are exhibited. Every distinguished visitor is given a guided tour of this museum by the proud managing director; and each year a special award is made to the team or individual who has contributed the most to Stroniron quality. Stroniron is experiencing financial problems. Everyone knows the reason why: no one will pay the prices for Stroniron quality – manufacturers who used to buy from them are looking for cheaper materials and less sophisticated design. The Stroniron board has often asked for the necessary changes, but somehow the new skills are not developed – and sales are decreasing while overheads remain high. No one, from the chief executive downwards, understands why this should be so.

The nature of rewards

Bearing these examples in mind we can begin to tease out
the factors which are at work. Let's start with the nature of
rewards.

I do not suppose that any manager who cares to reflect on
his experience is naive enough to think that money is either
the only reward, or is inevitably successful as a motivator. It
can of course be very powerful for those who are without
money, and need it to achieve a minimum standard of living;
and it can be powerful for those who feel that their status or
importance depends on their earning power or capital. It can
also be powerful negatively – many people are much more
influenced by the threat of loss of money than by the prospect of obtaining it. But for the generality of people who
earn a reasonable income money is often overtaken in
importance by other, and less tangible, rewards. I can well
remember being ambitious for my first sales management
job, but it was not the extra money that weighed with me – it
was the prospect of having an office to myself which attracted. If that would not have been a motivation for you, it only
shows that each of us is motivated differently.

There are different motivations at work in the examples
above. Jennifer's reward is the approbation she receives for
a particular piece of sales promotion – she likes the con-
gratulations, the letters of thanks from the sales force, the
admiration of her colleagues. It may be that there is something in her temperament which makes her particularly susceptible to this public recognition, but we do not need to
examine that – the need for admiration is common, to some
degree, to all of us. Similarly the satisfaction which Jennifer
derives from her personal involvement in her work – which
makes delegation difficult for her – is one which many will
recognize. The rewards available to the staff of Stroniron are
more subtle. Despite the fact that everyone recognizes the
need for change, the company is still implicitly rewarding the
good but old-fashioned design which is too expensive to sell.
The managing director can talk about modernizing products
from dawn till dusk but his eyes still say that the old way was
better, and his museum and annual awards are a witness to

this. We might imagine that a designer who started work on a modern design would be sensitive to the unspoken negative feelings of his colleagues; and there are a thousand ways of delaying or quashing new ideas, using every reason but the right one. In fact Stroniron is continuing to reward the old-fashioned and, as long as it does so, the old-fashioned is what it will get.

Hamish provides an example of a negative reward. (I use this term rather than punishment, which sounds too strong for this situation.) The first few minutes of trying to obtain time with his boss are an unpleasant experience; by avoiding the interview Hamish avoids the unpleasantness. He is, if you like, rewarded by this avoidance. Of course there are some people who are sufficiently assertive to ignore this, but Hamish is not one of them.

Thus rewards come in many shapes and sizes – money, power, status, social approval, self-fulfilment, intellectual pleasure, physical pleasure, sense of security, and so on. Under different circumstances the priority of rewards can change, and their degree of application and nature can vary with the circumstances and personality of the recipient. The manager who seeks to change or modify behaviour in problem solving and other contexts needs to understand rewards and to be sensitive to how they apply to each individual.

Learning about rewards

Hamish's story illustrates another point. We may suppose that the first few times he approached his boss he coped with the gruff, irritated reaction. As time passed, the association in his mind between contacting his boss and an unpleasant experience grew, and he gradually learnt that to avoid this he must keep away. In fact the boss, quite unintentionally, has been teaching Hamish to avoid him. When Hamish made his bad decision and his boss carpeted him over this, Hamish would have been quite justified in answering: 'It was you who taught me to keep away; now you're blaming me for learning the lesson.' But the boss wouldn't have understood, and Hamish himself may well not have realized the processes at work which have led to his behaviour.

A similar learning process has taken place in the other two examples. Stroniron staff have learnt throughout their time with the firm that conservatism is the rewarded attitude. It has come to them in positive ways – such as colleagues' reaction to old-fashioned design – and in negative ways through implicit disapproval of modern design. As in the case of Hamish, it may not be conscious. The managing director cannot understand why he does not get the changes he knows to be necessary, yet it is he who is giving the leadership in teaching the community that the old ways are best. It is previous experiences, no doubt, which have taught Jennifer that her personal involvement in her work is very satisfying, and that she takes less pleasure, or is even jealous, of her subordinates' success.

Reinforcing rewards

This feature of people learning through repeated instances about the rewards they receive is common. Even if we suppose that Jennifer first learnt the pleasures of admiration through the reaction to a single promotion, this will have been reinforced through repeating the experience. Indeed, if her succeeding promotions had been badly received she would gradually have lost the association between work and reward. Under some circumstances, learning can be reinforced even when the experience is not repeated. We could imagine Hamish having a first interview with his boss, and finding it an exceptionally unpleasant occasion. The next time he knows he should be consulting him he gets more and more anxious. At the last moment he finds an excuse for avoiding the consultation and making the decision himself. Once bitten, twice shy. His reward is the removal of his anxiety. And every time in future that he considers seeing his boss he gets a wobbly feeling in his tummy; and every time he decides that, after all, he doesn't need to go, the wobbly feeling disappears. And so the lesson that it is better to find reasons not to go is reinforced.

Intrinsic and extrinsic rewards

These thoughts lead us to a distinction between types of reward which is important for the Goal setting stage. Some rewards come from the very nature of an activity (intrinsic), and some come from outside (extrinsic). Jennifer is subject to both: her satisfaction in her personal involvement in the work is intrinsic – the pleasure comes from contemplating a job well done; the reward she gets from admiration is extrinsic – it comes from outside, and one could imagine circumstances in which it would not be forthcoming notwithstanding the quality of the work. One might imagine the designers at Stroniron, who were no doubt attracted to the firm because they had an inclination towards its design philosophy, receiving intrinsic reward from the traditional design, as well as the extrinsic reward of implicit approval.

If we consider this distinction in relation to the need to reinforce learning about rewards we can see an important point. A behaviour which gives an intrinsic reward is self-reinforcing. Every time Jennifer feels satisfaction her learning is reinforced; every time Hamish feels his anxiety leaving him his behaviour is reinforced. Behaviour which gives extrinsic rewards is dependent on those rewards continuing. If the field force lost patience with Jennifer's promotion programme, and withheld their admiration because of it, we would expect her gradually to unlearn the association between her work and the admiration received; if the managing director of Stroniron, having read this chapter, gradually changed the firm's approval for the old fashioned and promoted approval for the new, the staff would gradually unlearn the existing lesson, and recognize that the reward balance had changed. We will return to this point in a moment, but you can see the relevance to the choosing of goals which are intrinsically satisfying, and the provision of reinforcement if they are not.

A bird in the hand

I suggested at the beginning of this chapter that the balance of rewards was generally the deciding factor, and it may appear from my examples that this is really not so. The balance of rewards for Jennifer is surely in favour of her doing the complete task and retaining her job – with perhaps promotion and extra pay; Hamish must realize that the unpleasantness he associates with approaching his manager is trivial compared with the risk of making a bad decision; and Stroniron will eventually face liquidation for the want of a change which everyone knows is needed. Nor is this an unfamiliar outcome in other contexts – balance lung cancer and heart disease against the minor pleasure of lighting a cigarette and there is no contest, yet people smoke. There must be an invisible, yet very heavy, weight sitting on the scales to change the outcome. And there is: it is the weight of immediacy. Lung cancer and heart disease lie some time in the future, the pleasure of the cigarette is now. Jennifer's career development is in the future, applause comes today; Stroniron's liquidation remains remote until it is too late to avoid, rewards for traditional design are immediate.

Experts in human behaviour emphasize the power of immediate reward over long term benefit in motivation. It seems likely that this has been an important factor in the evolutionary success of our species. Nowadays this characteristic can still work for us; but it will work against us unless we learn to use it properly.

Summarizing rewards

Before turning to the application of all this to goal setting it will be helpful to summarize the main characteristics of rewards:

- Rewards are of many different kinds, and the priority a person gives them will depend on circumstances and temperament.

- Rewards may be positive or negative; a positive reward reinforces the behaviour leading to it, a negative reward discourages the behaviour.

- People learn to behave in certain ways (or to avoid behaving in certain ways) when experience leads them to associate that behaviour with its reward. Very often they do not realize this is happening. Similarly an individual can teach other people certain behaviours by reinforcing them with rewards. They may well not realize they are doing so.

- Rewards may be intrinsic or extrinsic. An intrinsic reward arises out of the behaviour itself, and is therefore always likely to be present; extrinsic reward comes from outside, and is incidental to the behaviour – it may or may not continue to be present.

- Behaviour which is not reinforced tends to lapse after a period.

- In weighing the balance of rewards great weight is put on immediacy; it is quite usual for human beings to sacrifice important long term benefits such as health or employment for the sake of immediate reward.

Matching rewards to the individual

Chris is quite a good salesman; he performs satisfactorily but not up to his full potential. Once a year his company holds a Chairman's Month, and a cup is awarded for the best performance. During this month Chris doubles his sales figures, and wins the cup. He scarcely knows the chairman, but he is motivated by the honour of winning. If he were truly motivated by money he would perform at a higher average level throughout the year; as it is he only steps up his performance for a cup which is worth only a fraction of the bonus he can earn through his sales success.

Carla works best in a structured situation. She once had her own business but it failed because she could not discipline herself to work. She hates letting people down, and she will work night and day to complete a job which someone expects of her by a certain date.

On the basis of these descriptions Chris and Carla are very different people, and are likely to need their goals structured in a different way. If we suppose that Chris has a goal to improve the volume of each sale he makes, it will be good if this can be recognized in some way. In order to help him his manager decides to publish the average size of sale per salesman on a monthly basis; Chris agrees that he would work hard to lead that list. For Carla it may be sufficient reward to know that her manager is expecting her to report on her completed goals in a month's time. She will not let her down.

Positive and negative

Ken is rather young and immature. In order to feel more important and masculine he swears a good deal, and this has become a habit. Some of the women in the works have complained about his language. In helping him set a goal for change, his manager considers negative reinforcement. This would take the form of Ken paying 50 pence to charity every time he swears. Alternatively, the manager wonders whether the greater acceptance of a Ken who has learnt not to swear would be a sufficient reward in itself.

The 'swearbox' penalty has often been used to good effect, and may well work here if Ken is really motivated, and enters into the spirit. But generally positive reinforcement is more effective than negative, and in this case would have the advantage of being self-sustaining. However, the effect may not be immediate, and Ken may lose heart before he sees a change in attitudes towards him. Can you think of a way in which he could achieve positive reinforcement immediately? If not, then perhaps both the methods under consideration could be used in concert.

Learning new behaviours

Meg has undertaken to make a list of her priority tasks every evening before she goes home. She reports after a week or two

that her performance has been patchy – when she completes
the goal she benefits, but all too often she is rushing for her train
and it doesn't get done. In the last few days she hasn't bothered
at all. In order to help her establish the habit her manager asks
her to complete a duplicate list using a carbon. She will put the
copy into his in-tray before she leaves. They agree to do this for
a month, and to see whether this proves long enough to make
the habit permanent.

Jennifer is looking for ways to reinforce her new goal of
supplying the sales force with a full sales promotion programme. She agrees to hold a written survey twice a year, on
which the salesmen can comment on the adequacy of the programme. It will also report on the action taken on their previous
suggestions. In this way the sales force will be keeping her up
to the mark and, she hopes, giving her satisfying recognition for
what she is doing.

Persistence is a problem we have looked at before. If the
achievement of a goal is truly adequate in itself persistence
may not be a problem. But if the goal does not have that
effect (Meg finds it more – immediately – rewarding to omit
her list; Jennifer still hankers for instant admiration) then
thought has to be given to strengthening and sustaining the
goal so that new habits and associations can be formed.
When Meg is praised for her efficiency, and Jennifer is made
aware of how she is contributing to sales success, a more
permanent reinforcement will be available. But it is not
surprising that behaviour which has been established over a
long period takes time to change.

Intrinsic and extrinsic

The drawback of extrinsic rewards is that they may not
always be available. Ken's swearbox may work as long as it's
kept up, but unless he is getting the intrinsic satisfaction
from learning that mature masculinity is found in con-
siderate behaviour, he will be prone to lapse into his old
habits. When Meg begins to see herself as a high achieving

businesswoman, and realizes that this depends on the efficient organization of her time, the intrinsic reward will be there and she will no longer need the extrinsic prompt of the discipline she has undertaken. Therefore in goal setting a manager should always look for goals which are intrinsically rewarding, although extrinsic reward will often be needed, especially in the early stages. However, the two will usually work well together.

> Helen (the market researcher whose reports were unreadably long) had adopted the goal of providing a two-page executive summary to head her reports. She quickly finds an intrinsic reward since the summaries help her to structure the body of the report more clearly; and she is proud of the neatness and clarity of the summaries. But she also has an extrinsic reward in that her manager will review her summaries, and will give her positive feedback on them.

Perhaps the most frequently used method for providing intrinsic and extrinsic rewards for a goal comes, quite simply, from pride in completing the goal (intrinsic), and the reward of positive feedback from demonstrating to the manager that the goal has been achieved. This is where immediacy is very much on the side of the goal-completer. The reward from reporting on achievement may be small, but it is definite and quick. This is one of the principles on which organizations like Weightwatchers or Alchoholics Anonymous rely. There is a strong motivation in being able to report success – stronger even than the long term benefits that the whole exercise is designed to achieve.

Rewards and the Exploration stage

We have been examining the nature of rewards and the value they can have in helping presenters to set goals which are likely to be achieved. But you will have noticed that these considerations can also be exceedingly valuable for the Exploration stage. When neither you nor the presenter is able to understand the reasons for behaviour – either that of the presenter or of others involved in the situation – it can often be valuable to explore the rewards being obtained. Sometimes what is apparently quite perverse behaviour can be explained in this way. The accounts of Jennifer and Hamish provide straightforward examples of this. For instance, Hamish's explanation that he preferred to make his own decisions rather than bother his boss sounds, taken at face value, rather thin. It is only when we see what is happening in terms of negative reward that we understand the problem, and have a basis for putting it right. Let's take two further examples to illustrate this. The first one will sound extreme to anyone not concerned with sales, but it will be very familiar to those who are:

> Graham sells advertising space on commission. He has a good selling manner on the telephone and no one can understand his mediocre performance. When his manager helps him analyse his work routines it is discovered that Graham will often hang on to a list of good prospective customers for two or three days before contacting them. This counterproductive activity is hard to explain. But eventually Graham has the insight to see that while his list is intact he feels comfortable – there is potential business there. But once he has contacted the list he feels he will have no future customers left, and this will cause him great anxiety.

The whole sales field is fertile ground for those wishing to understand rewards in action because their effect is often easier to observe than elsewhere. A successful sales career can depend on the ability of the individual to handle the balance of anxieties which drive him forward or hold him back. Here is a rather different example:

> Benjamin is employed in market analysis, and he does an excellent job. However, he is very critical of his company's unwillingness to take radical and effective steps – steps his analyses tell him are necessary. An opportunity for promotion comes up, and his boss, believing this will give Benjamin a real chance to bring about some of the changes he has advocated, discusses the new post with him. To the boss's surprise Benjamin shows

little enthusiasm and cannot make up his mind whether to apply for the post or not. After some mystification it transpires that Benjamin is happy in a job which allows him to express an opinion but saves him from taking responsibility; the new job will require him to stand up and be counted, and it will expose him to just the sort of criticism he has been making of others. Benjamin decides to stay where he is, but his better understanding of himself helps him to be a more constructive critic in the future.

And while we are in the area of marketing you will remember Helen who produced the voluminous reports no one would read. Might it be that she was getting her immediate reward from the comprehensiveness of her work, rather than the more appropriate reward which would be obtained from providing less thorough reports which were actually of use?

Rewards on a larger scale

Using the example of Stroniron I suggested that the whole atmosphere or culture of a company might be rewarding inappropriate behaviour. This is relevant to problem solving face to face because the individual with the problem may well be motivated by this culture without realizing it. Many problems cannot be solved in isolation, and need to be seen in the wider context of the whole company:

Mrs Carlton is the manager of a building society branch, and she is in difficulties because the volume of savings deposits attributable to her branch is low – and threatening the viability of her operation. At first sight this is strange because she has always had a good record for the obtaining of new accounts. When the situation is analysed in terms of rewards it seems that her area manager has always recognized and publicized success with obtaining new accounts. He has taken for granted the retention of existing accounts and, despite the importance of total volumes held, these receive much less publicity. So Mrs Carlton works hard to obtain new accounts, and trains her staff to do the same. Existing account holders are neglected, and have little encouragement to build up their deposits; and some of them, receiving unenthusiastic service, move their accounts elsewhere. Who is to blame: Mrs Carlton or her area manager? It doesn't matter; once the problem has been understood it can be corrected.

Gloucester Life Assurance Ltd was established at the beginning of the century. With a long reputation for reliability it has prospered, but now it is facing new markets and it is concerned about its ability to change with the times. It has an unspoken motto, built up over the decades: 'Gloucester Life doesn't make mistakes.' Everyone in the company is aware, at least subconsciously, that mistakes and failures get much more negative notice than successes get positive acclaim – and the way to the top is to keep your head down and your nose clean. Managers in Gloucester Life need to remember this characteristic whenever they discuss performance problems with staff. But of course they are part of the culture too, and may be no more aware of it than of the air they breathe.

Summary

- As a general rule people behave according to the way they see the balance of benefits accruing to them.

- However, the nature of the benefits, and the way they are balanced, does not always accord with our commonsense judgments. The characteristics of benefits are summarized on p. 155.

- This general rule is important in problem solving because it can be used in formulating goals and sub-goals which provide a favourable balance of benefits, and which therefore help the goal to be performed.

- It can also be useful at the Exploration stage when it explains behaviour which is apparently counterproductive or even perverse.

- It can be useful to remember that problem presenters are subject to the influence of company or group culture; sometimes this culture is actually rewarding counterproductive behaviour.

12　Underpinning

Underpinning is the assistance which the presenter may need to carry out his goals. It may take place away from the problem solving interview, and with the assistance of people other than the manager concerned. Examples would be training or organizational change. But, particularly when the increased skills needed are interpersonal, the manager may be teaching many of the skills he is using himself in problem solving. In suitable instances this will take place within the interview itself.

Underpinning is the fourth stage in the LEGUP problem solving model. The problem has been presented, often in a confused and emotional way, at the Listening stage. The manager has responded by absorbing the presenter's story and demonstrating that he has seen it from the presenter's perspective. Through this empathy, and the trust it develops, it has become possible to untangle the problem in the Exploration stage – to discover the core of the problem, and to establish who or what has to change in order to put matters right. But identifying the changes is academic unless the goals for change are defined in a way which gives them a maximum chance of success, and the presenter is prepared to commit himself to achieving them. This is the task of the Goal setting stage. Yet in many instances another stage has to be accomplished before the goals can be tackled. The reasons for this may be obvious both to manager and presenter, but they are systematically revealed by the use of the pushmepullyou chart, described on p. 39. This chart, you will recall, helped the problem solvers to identify the factors in the circumstances which would help the goals to be achieved, and those which would hinder.

A background example

Walter has chosen the goal of achieving better delegation to his staff. But, amongst other factors, he has identified three difficulties relevant to the Underpinning stage. One is that he is not entirely sure that the long term advantages of delegation outweigh the short term nuisances of briefings and delay; the second is that his communication skills for delegation are not very good – he finds it hard to imagine what it is like for one of his subordinates to receive instructions from him; the third is that he believes that his boss, Mr Simkins, will only accept work done in a particular way – a way that Walter cannot expect his staff to master.

In order to help Walter to achieve his goal these difficulties must be reduced or removed, and this is a typical task for the Underpinning stage. It is discouraging, and ultimately pointless, to attempt a goal for which one is not properly prepared.

Walter provides an example of three different kinds of underpinning need. The first is motivational – how do I convince myself that delegation is worth the trouble?; the second is concerned with a skill – how do I communicate my instructions accurately?; the third requires him to investigate, and perhaps change, the attitude of another person. At this stage the manager must decide whether the underpinning can be given as part of the problem solving process, or whether it must be provided in some other way. In this instance the manager decides that he can give some help straight away, although outside assistance may also prove to be needed.

Walter's manager recognizes that his uncertainty over whether delegation is worth the time and trouble constitutes a mini problem, and so he decides to use the LEGUP routine. Walter talks about his feelings, and his manager helps him to explore. They discover that the source of Walter's hesitation is not the practical difficulties of delegation (this is just a rationalization) but Walter's fear of having to take responsibility for work which has been done by someone other than himself. However, he accepts that, if his delegation were successful, he would have more confidence in the outcome. Thus the goal for solving the first difficulty turns out to be improving his delegation skills – which is what he has already identified as his second need.

To help him with this his manager suggests that Walter changes his frame of reference in order to see the process from the staff point of view. He asks Walter to act out (role play) being a member of staff while he, the manager, takes Walter's part and describes a job he wants done. When they discuss this afterwards Walter is able to recognize the difficulties involved in receiving instructions, and to see the principles which need to be observed for delegation to be really effective. Walter thinks he will need more training and practice to master this, but already he feels he could do a much better job through his new understanding.

The Simkins problem already sounds a little easier, too, since Walter's developing delegation skills will enable his staff to achieve higher standards. However, it will still be necessary to speak to him, and get him to cooperate with Walter's delegation plans. Here the manager is able to help by asking Walter to rehearse what he might say to Simkins, and how he might deal with Simkins' possible reactions.

While they are both happy with progress so far, they agree that Walter needs further training in delegation skills. The manager suggests that Walter should consult the personnel director about this. Walter agrees, and he asks the manager to have a word with Mr Simkins, to smooth the path. The manager is not sure whether this is a good idea.

You will have noticed that in this example the manager has drawn on the battery of skills he uses for problem solving in order to carry out the underpinning task. This is no coincidence: time and again the skills we have been discussing come to the manager's aid in so many aspects of his work.

But, of course there will also be underpinning tasks which cannot be part of the problem solving interview. I would like to discuss some of these at this point, and return to the adaptation of problem solving skills to the Underpinning stage later in the chapter.

Help from outside

In the case of Walter the manager was able to make some progress in increasing delegation skills there and then. But, as Walter recognized, this would not be enough: more instruction would be needed. It would be the task of the manager to make sure that this instruction or training was available to Walter. This does not mean that he necessarily needs to choose, say, an external course and enrol Walter. Since one of the objects of the LEGUP method is to enable the presenter to become more self-sufficient the manager may well be asking him to look out an appropriate course for himself, or to seek help directly from the personnel department – as he does in this case. Choosing the right course and succeeding at it may well become a sub-goal like any other. Several of the examples used in this book imply the need for training:

> Beryl (p. 14) was willing to take on more demanding tasks in her department provided she received training. Her manager arranges for a senior member of the department to undertake this.

> Roger (p. 61) was getting poor sales figures. It was established that his ratio of sales to sales interviews was poor – a result of his bad closing technique. Roger undertakes to have some training in this so that he can achieve his targets.

Smoothing the path

Walter is going to speak to Mr Simkins about his delegation plans, and enlist his cooperation. Should the manager take a hand here – particularly since Walter asked him to? Once

again the bias should be towards encouraging the presenter
to see the job through. But there could well be circumstances in which the manager could lend a hand, and opportunities like this are quite frequent:

> Drake (p. 61) is having problems persuading the company
> accountant that his purchase of new computer equipment will
> be cost effective. Although he has developed a strategy for
> bringing the accountant round to his point of view his manager
> might be able to help by talking the problem over with the
> accountant directly. This tactic should be considered.

> Helen (p. 129) is setting about her sub-goals of making her
> market intelligence reports more attractive to read. But she
> realizes that her reputation for indigestible writing may prevent
> the recipients from realizing she has changed her ways, since
> they may not bother to read her improved reports. Among the
> ways to solve this difficulty is that her manager should persuade
> the recipients directly to look at Helen's next report in a new
> light.

There is a danger of manipulation here. If the manager acts
in this way without telling the presenter, he is actually rig-
ging the outcome in advance, and the presenter will be
getting an artificial response when he takes his own action.
In general this is not desirable, but it is possible to imagine
situations in which, exceptionally, a manager might consider
this justified. The alternative – of asking the presenter
beforehand whether he wishes this help – contains another
danger: some presenters would always prefer to have their
problems solved for them, while their manager would prefer
them to develop their independence. Good judgement is
needed.

Executive action

Many business problems cannot be solved by the action of
the presenter alone. Sometimes they will have arisen as a
result of some factor which is not in the control of the
presenter but may be in the control of the manager:

Margaret (p. 117) and her manager conclude that the problem of absenteeism in her department could be helped if the school leavers were seasoned with a higher proportion of experienced staff. This is a matter of company policy, and to bring it about Margaret's manager must take action.

One of your junior staff is at loggerheads with her section leader. She has tried to sort this out without success. You decide to ask both parties to come and see you together so that a mutually acceptable solution can be found.

Once again the manager must avoid pressure from the presenter to use his authority to change the situation in a way which will solve the problem without further effort on the presenter's part. Such a decision should be taken only when it is a necessary element in the solution. Equally there is an opposite temptation – to avoid interference when this may be the only way of solving a problem with reasonable despatch:

John Serbo, the managing director, has two divisional managers who always seem to be bickering over the overlap of their responsibilities. Both have raised this difficulty with him privately. Because they are intelligent he thinks they ought to be able to sort it out between them. And since they are both strong personalities he is nervous about taking action directly. If he appears to favour one the other may be put out; if he invites both of them to discuss it together with him, there may be painful conflict. So he does nothing; and, meanwhile, energy and time is wasted over a squabble that might have been sorted out quite quickly through firm executive action.

Underpinning in the interview

When we looked at the underpinning which Walter required in order to achieve his objectives, it seemed possible that it might, at least partially, be provided within the interview itself. I suggested that it was no coincidence that the skills which might be used for this were often the same skills required generally for good problem solving. If you glance back at the summaries of the earlier chapters of this book, particularly those dealing with the Exploration stage, you will see that quite a number of skills have been described. In looking at how these might be used for underpinning, I will only select a few to act as representatives of the others; and I will add one or two more which would not ordinarily be used in the earlier stages of the LEGUP process.

Of course underpinning of this type might well take place on a separate occasion. You will see that the nature of the methods requires them not to be hurried; they usually require some internal change on the part of the presenter, and it is not possible to force the pace unduly.

Use of the LEGUP process

When Walter expressed some reluctance over delegation his manager recognized it as a mini-problem and applied the LEGUP process. It often happens that, at the Goal setting stage, the presenter begins to get cold feet. He has followed willingly through the Exploration stage, accepting the reasonableness of all that has been discovered. Faced by a goal or sub-goal, he sees reality approaching fast, and unresolved doubts begin to appear. Sometimes these doubts are expressed directly, but the experienced manager will be using his skills in non-verbal communication. I spoke about the importance of these in Chapter 4. Signs of doubt or anxiety should be tactfully investigated, and it may be revealed that the presenter, while accompanying the manager intellectually through the process, has left his emotions behind somewhere along the way. Then, as happened with Walter, it is necessary to go back over the LEGUP process to trace and understand the difficulty, so that it can be put right. Going back over the LEGUP process, or back to an earlier stage, is frequently needed – either when a new problem comes to the surface (see p. 19) or, as in this case, when it turns out that the presenter has not fully accepted the completion of an earlier stage.

Learning to be a good listener

The skills of good listening, which I emphasized so strongly in earlier chapters, were examined from the point of view of the manager, who needed to use them at the Listening stage (and throughout the process). But goals will often be chosen for which the presenter will need them too. In fact, any goal which involves meeting and discussion with another person – but particularly when there is some disagreement to be resolved – will require good listening for its proper accomplishment.

You will recall that the deep listening which enabled you to put your whole attention to the other person, helped you to see the picture from his point of view, and led to you communicating your understanding through mirror summaries, was a powerful tool. It quickly built up trust and confidence, enabling the speaker to express his real concerns. You can see that if this is valuable in problem solving it will also help the presenter when he is in dialogue with someone else. Indeed the difficulty to be solved may well have arisen through the people concerned not being skilled at listening to each other:

> John Serbo's divisional managers, who bickered about the overlap of their responsibilities, had in fact made a number of efforts to work harmoniously. But when they met they did not really listen to each other – they were each too concerned to protect his own point of view. Although some of these meetings ended with apparent agreement nothing really changed: there was no trust, no confidence, no understanding.

Ideally one would like to help both of these divisional managers to listen better. But even teaching just one of them may eventually lead to harmony because good listening is infectious. If someone listens to you well it is natural to reciprocate. The whole atmosphere of the exchange will often have moved from one of confrontation to one of attempted mutual understanding. The skilled listener acts as a model for the other, who begins to pick up the elements of good listening unconsciously.

This fact is also helpful in teaching the presenter to use good listening as a preparation for carrying out an agreed goal. The manager has acted as a model for good listening throughout the LEGUP process, and the presenter may already have increased his skills through imitation. It is then relatively easy for the manager to explain the skills of good listening in terms of the example he has given, and then to invite the presenter to practise these consciously in dialogue with him.

Rehearsal

Before undertaking a goal which involves dialogue over a contentious matter, and which will involve good listening, it can be valuable for the presenter to have tried to understand, at quite a deep level, the point of view of the other party.

> Lilian (p. 96) has decided that she is going to talk directly to the personnel director about how she would like to fit into the new company reorganization. She realizes that he may be touchy about the subject. Her manager pretends that she is Lilian, and Lilian plays the personnel director. They carry out the conversation in these roles, and through doing so Lilian gains a much better understanding of the personnel director's likely point of view, and how she can best cope with it.

In this case rehearsal was used to change a frame of reference. We saw another example of this when Walter was asked to put himself into the position of one of his staff receiving instruction. But it can also be used directly to prepare the presenter for what he may have to say. For instance, Lilian could also have worked the other way round. Her manager would have played the personnel director, and she would have played herself – practising her message, and preparing herself to deal with various responses. Of course it is difficult to guess how other people will react in a conversation, but – even when it does not work out in the way foreseen, the practice somehow prepares and sensitizes the mind for optimum action. This use of rehearsal is valuable for the achievement of so many goals that I will provide some more examples to give a flavour of the variety of occasions when it can be used.

> The executive who wanted to be more open in expressing his opinion at meetings (Goal 1, p. 144) decided he would tick his pad to record how often he has succeeded in his goal. But he is nervous about how to express himself when he disagrees with the consensus of his colleagues. His manager asks him to think up a few typical situations, and then to practise what he would say. Initially his statements come out awkwardly and belligerently; it is easy to foresee his colleagues' reaction. But with rehearsal he learns how to make his points positively, and in a way which will attract a sensible hearing.

> Roger and his manager know there is something wrong with his closing technique which is losing him many sales. In order to pinpoint this his manager asks him to go back over the dialogue of his last interview. It turns out that his customer was on the point of buying when Roger backed off, and lost his moment. His manager role plays Roger, and demonstrates how he could have closed the sale at that point. Then he asks Roger to try again, with the manager playing the customer.

> Victor, who is the marketing manager, has a problem. He has given the impression to a number of people that he does not welcome new ideas. This arises from the fact that, for practical reasons, he can only use a tiny proportion of the ideas for products and promotions which are fed to him by his colleagues; and he has fallen into the habit of pouring cold water onto the suggestions he receives. He discusses with his director ways in which he can react to ideas and sound positive about them, even if few can be used. His director puts a few possible ideas to him, and Victor practises his new response until it begins to feel natural to him.

Non-verbal communication

Non-verbal communication, an important skill for the manager, may also be an important skill for the presenter. It is difficult to teach quickly, and it takes time, as you will have discovered, to practise and develop. But there will be occasions when a presenter can be helped by some guidance here:

Prescott has an interesting problem. Although he is quite senior he is always being interrupted when he is trying to say something. He finds this very irritating, and it has led to harsh words with his subordinates. His manager listens to Prescott's explanation and begins to see what is happening. When people ordinarily finish what they have to say, and give space to others to enter the conversation, they indicate this by their tone of voice, speed of speech and their gestures. Prescott is in the habit of using these signals whenever he is pausing for thought. Naturally others take these cues in the usual way, and start speaking. Using a tape recorder the manager demonstrates this to Prescott, who now can see the problem clearly. They then practise and experiment so that Prescott can learn how to give the cues he intends.

Ralph is a good salesman, and a charming, well liked man. But he has never been very successful using the telephone. Anyone who has spoken to him on the telephone could tell him why. For some unexplained reason all his charm goes; he comes over as hurried, gruff and bad tempered. It seems that the telephone flusters him, and his tension communicates itself through his voice. When they have explored the problem, and Ralph has heard what he sounds like for himself, his manager suggests that when using the telephone he should force himself to smile, just as if he were talking face to face. It sounds silly to Ralph, but he discovers that it is difficult to smile and be tense at the same time; somehow the smile lightens his voice and improves the whole effect of what he is saying.

Lightning lessons

You will have noticed that most of the examples I have been using have involved the manager in providing some training in a skill which the presenter needs in order to achieve an objective. Because managerial time is short such training needs to be as efficient as possible. The simple framework which follows may help you.

Imagine a tennis professional teaching you a new stroke. You would expect him to work in four simple stages. First, he would explain the stroke – what it's used for, the grip needed, the path of the racquet, and so on. Second, he would demonstrate or model the stroke so that you could see it in action. Third, he would ask you to practise the stroke. And fourth, he would review your attempts. He might need to go through this sequence a number of times: Explanation, Demonstration, Practice, Review, before you were comfortable with the new skill.

Exactly the same sequence is required for teaching the skills which are needed to underpin a chosen goal:

As Roger and his manager discuss the last interview when Roger failed to close business, they discover that, after Roger has made his sales presentation, he just sits back waiting for his customer to make an order. 'I don't want to rush him,' says Roger. 'If I'm too pushy he'll go on the defensive. Besides, if my presentation is good, he really ought to buy without further prompting.'

The manager explains that customers rarely volunteer orders, they have to be eased into them gently. When Roger is satisfied that he has given the right information to obtain the order he should proceed on the assumption that it will go through smoothly. He should be giving the customer choices about the order, while filling in the details on the order form – taking it for granted that the order itself will be made. (Explanation)

The manager then demonstrates the technique in action: 'Have I covered all the points you had in mind, Mr Jones? Good. Now tell me, which is most convenient for you – the two kilogram bags, or the ten-kilogram sacks? The sacks? OK. I can either arrange for three months' supply, or for six months'. On six months' supply there's an automatic 10 per cent discount. Which would you prefer?' (Demonstration)

Roger is then asked to practise the technique using a number of variations on this implied consent, while his manager role plays the customer. (Practice)

He carries this out well but, in his concentration on the words, he forgets to complete the order form. His manager points this

out, explaining the importance of this element (Review). With
this explanation he starts the training sequence again, and this
time Roger does it right.

I have suggested that there might be occasions when the
presenter needed training in listening skills. You may, as an
exercise, like to pause and consider how you would use this
sequence for a lightning lesson.

Of course, this method of training is valuable in many
contexts other than the underpinning of goals for problem
solving. But some managers are apprehensive about the
demonstrations or modelling which is an intrinsic part of the
process. Most people who know their job are happy about
demonstrating ordinary skills – the tennis coach demonstrating a forehand smash, the accountant demonstrating
double entry book keeping. But few of us feel we are natural
actors, and the confidence to model a verbal skill is often
lacking. In fact it is not as difficult as our nervousness
suggests to us. With practice the skills of modelling can
usually be developed to an adequate degree; and it does not
need to be too high – otherwise the presenter may well feel
inhibited by the standard he is apparently being expected to
achieve. But in the end the fact has to be faced: we cannot
properly ask one of our staff to attempt something we are
not willing to do ourselves. Where verbal and relationship
skills are concerned, this is as much part of our job as
demonstrating a forehand smash is part of the job of the
tennis coach.

Summary

- It is important to ensure that the presenter is reasonably capable of achieving the chosen goals. A device
  such as the pushmepullyou chart will help here.

- Some of the assistance needed will be provided apart
  from the problem solving interview, e.g. training sessions, negotiating with people on the presenter's
  behalf, organizational change.

- As far as possible the presenter's independence should be encouraged by inviting him to undertake or organize the help he needs for himself. But the manager must be ready to take executive action when this is necessary.

- When the skill or preparation required is interpersonal the manager will find that the skills of problem solving are useful.

- Some difficulties which only come to light when the presenter is contemplating a goal constitute mini-problems for which LEGUP is appropriate.

- The manager will often need to teach the presenter skills he has himself been displaying in problem solving, e.g. good listening, changing the frame of reference, rehearsal, non-verbal communication.

- In giving such training efficiently the manager should remember the lightning lesson: Explanation, Demonstration, Practice, Review.

13   Pursuit

In the Pursuit stage the manager follows through the com-pletion of goals and sub-goals; he is checking that the agreed action has taken place and is working. He provides the reward of recognition for success, help with managing the goal strategy as it moves from step to step, and help with analysis and remedial action if goals are not achieved.

We have left the presenter with agreed goals and sub-goals which will, it is planned, bring about the best solution to the original problem. The necessary underpinning has been supplied and so we have every reason to be confident about the outcome. But the final stage – Pursuit – must not be omitted; it is an important and integral part of the LEGUP process. Ensuring that the goals have been completed and the problem actually solved will of course be important to the effective manager. He has no intention of devoting time to a problem and then neglecting to discover whether he has been successful. LEGUP is action-centred – it can only be judged by the observable changes in behaviour which put matters right. It is not concerned with aspiration but with accomplishment. We would think it very strange if a coach trained his athletes to the highest standard and then showed no concern with whether they won their races or not. The manager who is not interested in ensuring the goals are accomplished is just like that – he is interested in the process and not in the objective of the process. But in addition to this primary need the Pursuit stage helps directly with the completion of the goal strategy. It does so in three ways:

- His recognition that goals have been completed provides a valuable reward which helps the presenter to persist until the problem is solved.

- He is able to coach the presenter through the goal strategy; he checks that earlier goals have been satisfactorily completed, and that underpinning for later goals is provided.

- If a goal has not been accomplished, or attempted, the reasons can be established and further action taken.

Arranging for pursuit

The last action of the Goal setting stage was to arrange for follow up occasions or meetings to monitor or judge goals (p. 146). The intervals allowed will naturally vary according to circumstances, but when they are likely to be longer than a week thought should be given to the value of an intervening contact in order to monitor progress or provide encouragement. It is all too easy for the presenter to become discouraged unless he is urged into action by knowing that his manager is fully behind him, and interested in his progress.

The reward of recognition

In Chapter 11 we looked at rewards, and we noticed that rewards tend to work best when they are received quickly – on the heels of the achievement. In the case of some goals this is not a difficulty:

> Marilyn has a problem laying her hands on information and papers she needs. She has decided to solve this by reorganizing her filing system with the help of her secretary. She gets great satisfaction from doing this, and immediately feels the benefit to her work from the convenience of the new system.

Marilyn's goal turns out to be immediately self-reinforcing –
but often this is not so. Jennifer (p. 149), who is setting out
to provide a comprehensive sales promotion programme,
must expect the rewards from this to be delayed. Roger has
set himself the task of raising the proportion of sales interviews which results in completed sales, but it may be several
weeks before an improved trend can be clearly observed.
Without a more immediate reward there is a danger that
neither Jennifer nor Roger will succeed. And, as I have
already suggested, the most commonly used and convenient
reward is the acknowledgement by someone important of a
job well done.

Why are simple acknowledgements so effective? Often we
only realize their importance when they are absent. I am in
the habit of sending a brief note of thanks to any staff
member who has completed a worthwhile job; I rarely hear
about these notes again – but I always hear when I have
omitted to send one. And all of us have had occasions when
we were at least momentarily upset when no one recognized
that we had done well. One could argue that such acknowledgements are cheap – only words, but this is not true since
they carry the message that the acknowledger genuinely
cares. And that's not cheap at all; in a sense it's priceless.

So it is important that we demonstrate our real interest in
a presenter's success by ensuring that we have an opportunity to hear and acknowledge the outcome of a goal. For the
presenter this is a worthwhile and powerful immediate
reward. And there is an additional negative reward which
can also be motivating – the reluctance of the presenter to
admit that he has let the manager down.

Halfway house

The reward of acknowledgement can be particularly important when a goal is taking a long time to achieve:

> Jennifer has now decided that she will concentrate on providing
> a comprehensive sales promotion programme for the field
> force. Inevitably it will be a long time before they fully appreci-
> ate this. So her manager makes sure he reviews her progress

frequently, thus providing her with the reward of his approval to bridge the gap.

Recognizing achievement

An eminent sales manager of my acquaintance who is responsible for a field force of around a thousand salesmen tells me that every month he writes to or telephones several dozen people whose achievement is worth noting. While it is significant that he devotes so much time to this task, it is particularly interesting that every letter, however short, is different. When I asked him why, he said: 'When someone gets my letter he needs to know that I was thinking of him personally, and his performance, when I was writing it. Of course I could have my secretary do the whole thing using a series of form letters – it would save me hours of effort. But then they wouldn't be worth the postage stamp.'

This principle can be illustrated by two contrasting examples:

Manager: Did you get to that refresher course on closing sales, Roger?

Roger: Yes, I did. It finished last Thursday.

Manager: That's good. Well done. See you when you come in next week.

and

Manager: That's good. Well done. Did you find out what was going wrong?

Roger: Yes, I think so. My basic mistake seemed to be that I was waiting for the customer to volunteer an order, rather than using implied consent.

Manager: And have you had a chance to try that out in the field?

Roger: Not yet. But I'm seeing Brownlows this afternoon. That's going to be my first opportunity.

Manager: Well, good luck then. If you've got a moment, ring me and tell me how you got on.

Coaching the presenter through the goal strategy

Where a presenter has a number of sub-goals to complete he may be needing help of four kinds. The first is by way of reward and encouragement, as I have explained earlier; the second is to ensure that the earlier goals have been properly completed, and have done the job expected of them; the third is to modify or replace goals which have turned out to be unsatisfactory; and the fourth is to prepare for the next goals to come.

In providing a full acknowledgement for the completion of a goal in the way I have described it will incidentally help to establish whether the goal was satisfactorily completed or not. The manager needs to check three main factors:

1   Was the goal properly seen through to its conclusion?

2   Did it match up to any measurement agreed for judging its success?

3   Did it solve the problem or, in the case of a sub-goal, did it put the presenter in a position to move to the next sub-goal?

If the answers to these questions are satisfactory then the problem has been solved, or – when there is a hierarchy of sub-goals – the next step can be tackled. But if the goal has not been achieved, or has not given the expected benefit, closer probing will be needed in order to establish future action. But, assuming that the goal has been completed satisfactorily, consideration may need to be given to the next goal in the strategy.

Preparing for the next goal

Helen's first sub-goal is to produce a two-page summary of her report. She shows you this, and, after you have reviewed it together, you both agree that it covers the essence of the report succinctly and well. She then reminds you that her second sub-goal is to shorten the body of the report. But she needs to discuss this with you again because her concentration on the summary has put out of her mind a number of ideas on shortening you both discussed. You go through this together, agree the approximate percentage she aims to shorten it by, and agree the date when she will show you the result.

At the previous meeting you had both settled on a strategy to solve Helen's problem of getting her reports read and acted upon by senior management. There were a number of sub-goals leading up to this. But, as I have suggested, it is important to concentrate on one or two steps at a time. This means that the later sub-goals may only have been outlined at the Goal setting stage. But once an earlier goal has been completed it will be necessary to focus concentration on the next goal in the way this example demonstrated. Thus one important practical function of the Pursuit stage is to help in the management of the chosen goal strategy, remembering that the achievement of the earlier goal will provide a strong reinforcing motivation for taking on the next one. And this is a further reason for probing the goal; if it was never really accomplished the next sub-goal is even less likely to succeed, and the manager needs to know why.

Other kinds of underpinning may also be required:

You have been wondering whether you really have the time to give Helen advice about shortening her reports. A colleague has mentioned an excellent book on the subject which he has used, and you suggest to Helen that she might study this, and use her next sub-goal as a way of practising what she has learnt. You would not suggest this route to everyone but you know that Helen will respond well to private study, and will work hard at mastering the skill.

Dealing with uncompleted goals

There can be several reasons why a goal has not been completed, and establishing which one applies is a necessary guide to the next action which needs to be taken. The reasons can be listed under seven headings:

1   The opportunity to perform the goal has not occurred.

2   The goal was poorly chosen and could not be accomplished.

3   The strategy was poorly chosen and the steps are too large.

4   The presenter needed more underpinning to succeed.

5   The situation has changed and the problem has gone.

6   The presenter has changed and the problem has gone.

7   The presenter's motivation or confidence turns out to be insufficient.

Lack of opportunity

There is of course normally no problem when a goal has been delayed for lack of opportunity or the time to carry it out. It may be worth noticing whether this is likely to be a continuing practical difficulty – for instance Roger may be finding it impossible to get the time to go on his sales training refresher course – and, if so, to take the required action. More critical is the situation when the manager suspects that the practical problems are really a mask for faintheartedness – typified by this exaggerated dialogue:

Roger: I couldn't fit the training course into my schedule.

Manager: Couldn't you have put off some less important things and made space?

Roger: Yes, but it would have put me behind, and I'd never have caught up.

Manager: Surely someone would have covered for you meanwhile?

Roger: Yes, but no one else really knows my customers well enough.

Manager: Would two days away have really made any difference – after all you take your annual holiday?

Roger: Yes, but then I have time to warn customers first.

Manager: Couldn't you have dropped them a note and then gone on a course the following month?

Roger: Yes, but the training centre closes down for August, so there wouldn't be a course running.

You will have recognized the presence of a pattern. Each reason appears to hold up by itself but, taken together, the most credulous manager might be forgiven for suspecting that there is some other reason why the course has not been attended. And if you fail to challenge the pattern you may have relieved Roger of undertaking a goal that he really wants to avoid.

The poorly chosen goal

Margaret: I took the opportunity at the weekly department meeting to talk to the staff about their importance to the company. But they looked really bored, and I'm sure they thought I was just pushing the party line.

Manager: Did you give it another try?

Margaret: I didn't think I could really repeat myself. But I did try once or twice to bring the subject up in conversation. All they did was to switch off.

Manager: What d'you think was the trouble?

Margaret: Maybe they're just not that concerned about the company. And they're certainly not going to think differently just because I say it's important.

Manager: So it sounds as though that goal just isn't going to work. Maybe we should try and find another way of tackling the problem.

Goals are chosen because they seem at the time they are set to be attainable and useful. But inevitably some will turn out badly, and they will need to be modified. You will have noticed that her manager probed her initial failure in order to ensure that Margaret had made a real effort to succeed, and had not just given up after a halfhearted first attempt. In fact he might have probed a little more deeply – perhaps asking about what she had actually said. This might have revealed that the difficulty lay in the way in which she had presented the subject, rather than in the goal itself.

The steps are too large

The eagerness of the participants can lead to a choice of initial sub-goals which the presenter finds are too difficult to accomplish. This can be unfortunate if the failure leads to a loss of confidence – just as success would have led to an increase of confidence. However the remedy is straight-forward: split the sub-goals into smaller steps which can be accomplished more easily:

Helen brings you her first attempt at a two-page summary of her report. She is apologetic because it's seven pages long. She explains that she felt she really couldn't do justice even to the essence of the report in any shorter space. You ask her to accept an intermediate goal – to discipline herself to produce a list of no more than ten headings as though they were a contents page for the report. When she has done this she will have a clearer idea of the structure of the report; and you will be able to show her how to expand the the first two or three headings into a brief précis, leaving her to complete the remainder.

More underpinning needed

Walter: Actually it was pretty disastrous. I thought I'd try out my delegation by getting Greta to do the layout for the photos on the centrespread of the magazine. I explained it all in great detail. And, would you believe it, she didn't pick a single photo of the chairman and his wife. I had to start all over again – I was working till nearly nine so that the printers could have it in the morning.

Manager: I see what you mean. Mr Simkins would have turned in his grave if the magazine had been printed like that – and he's not even dead. Did you tell Greta that the chairman looks for pictures of himself first, and anyone else afterwards, long afterwards?

Walter: Well, no I didn't. I mean I should have thought that was obvious.

Manager: It doesn't seem to have been obvious to Greta. Tell me, she's not been with us long, has she? I doubt if she's ever met the chairman.

Walter: You mean I shouldn't have expected her to know that the chairman matters?

Manager: Maybe so. Perhaps we ought to talk a little more about the assumptions one can afford to make when delegating – particularly to someone who's very inexperienced.

This conversation suggested that Walter had experimented with delegation before he had mastered one of the basic techniques – and his manager is about to take the opportunity to give him some extra training. This is not surprising since no training can prepare people for every eventuality; and it can often happen that the need for more skills is only discovered through the practical experience of finding them wanting. And other kinds of additional underpinning may also turn out to be required. For instance, Roger's refresher course on closing more sales may not prove to be enough and his manager may have to suggest something further, like Roger pairing with a more experienced salesman for a few days.

The situation has changed and the problem has gone

Sometimes problems go away on their own, and obviously there's no point in completing goals to achieve a solution which already exists. But caution is needed. A problem can disappear temporarily, only to recur:

One of your managers was having real difficulty in motivating a member of staff, and he chose a goal which involved asking him to take some extra responsibility. But before he had put this into

action the staff member suddenly perked up and began to work
well. The goal was abandoned. But a month later the old problem was back; nothing had really been solved.

Perhaps in this instance your manager might have carried his
goal through – and he could have presented it to the staff
member as a recognition of his improving work effort. But
he certainly should have been ready for the possibility of
relapse. So you must be ready for the situation when the
presenter who is for some reason reluctant to attempt the
goal tells you that the problem has gone away. This can be
another instance when self-deception is at work.

The presenter has changed and the problem has gone

I can never make up my mind whether this outcome is
gratifying or frustrating. But it happens often enough. A
problem can come to a head as a result of a number of
coincident factors. The pressure brings the presenter to you,
and you set about helping to solve the problem. But the very
activity of articulating the problem has relieved the pressure.
The presenter is able to stand back and see the difficulties in
a new way. Maybe they now don't seem to be so difficult,
and the presenter decides he can live with them. Maybe a
more relaxed attitude enables him to handle the situation
better, and that leads to a solution. The presenter can of
course be aware of such changes early in the LEGUP process (see p. 54), and let the manager know. But it may be
that he does not fully realize what has happened until some
time has passed, or his new attitudes have been put into
action. It can be irritating for the manager to discover that
he has gone through all the later stages unnecessarily, but at
least there is the consolation that the problem has been
solved. However, the presenter's assurance that the problem
has gone away needs to be probed to make sure that wishful
thinking is not an element. And there may be opportunities
to reinforce the changes in the presenter, to help them
develop further and to persist.

Motivation or confidence turns out to be lacking

It is rare for a presenter to return at the Pursuit stage and
say: 'I didn't complete the objective because it didn't seem
worth all the hassle in order to solve my problem.' That this
may be the case is likely only to emerge as a result of probing
the apparently more respectable reasons which are initially
given for not completing a goal. But let's look at an example
of lack of motivation:

> June has felt for a long time that her work has never been
> appreciated because she is a woman. She feels she has to work
> much harder than her male colleagues to gain recognition.
> Having just joined your staff from another part of the company
> she has taken an early opportunity to raise the problem with
> you. From her account she certainly seems to have a point, and
> you both agree on some goals which will put matters right. And,
> being her boss, you will be in a strong position to help. But,
> somewhat to your surprise, she does not complete her objec-
> tives and, while she has plenty of excuses, there seems no good
> reason for this. You mention the incident to the colleague on
> whose staff June was previously. It turns out that he had exactly
> the same experience. You begin to wonder whether June gets
> some secret satisfaction from her righteous indignation at being
> overlooked. If that is so she dare not complete goals which may
> remove her problem. It's too precious to her.

June's behaviour seems perverse, but it is by no means
unusual. We can understand it better by remembering that,
in the balance of rewards, the immediate is likely to take
precedence over the remote. There are people who parade
the chip on their shoulder as a badge of identity; take it
away, and they disappear. And the chip is confirmed by
making attempts to remove it through raising it as a problem, sometimes with a succession of people. Every time the
problem fails to get solved (and they make sure,
unconsciously, that this *is* every time) it is another piece of
evidence that the chip is justified, and the identity gratify-
ingly secure. It reminds me of a busy doctor friend of mine
whose young family seems to suffer endlessly from minor

ailments. Who wants to get better when being ill is the only way you get attention from Dad? Who wants to remove the feeling that they are a victim of prejudice if this means they may have to face up to the fact that it is their own limitations which hold them back?

Once June's problem has been recognized, a skilled manager may be confident enough to challenge her. This may lead to June accepting her motivation and deciding to take positive steps to change it, or she may not be able to admit an interpretation which touches her so closely. She may feel insulted, and leave. If the challenge seems too risky the manager may decide to do nothing. If June's work is good and the chip not too intrusive this may be acceptable.

An example of lack of confidence

Gil was determined to be more assertive in expressing his opinions at meetings. He decided on his goals and spent some time with his manager practising what he might say and how to say it. When he reported at the Pursuit stage the results looked very thin. Gil finally admitted that he hadn't actually tried out any of the ideas. When his manager invited him to examine and perhaps modify his goal Gil looked uneasy and sounded unenthusiastic. Further discussion revealed that, faced by action, Gil had lost all his motivation. He now felt that he just wasn't the sort of person to assert himself, and he believed he would never overcome his fear.

Lost on voyage

LEGUP is not infallible. Not every problem is soluble, and sometimes it will be necessary to settle for compromise improvements, or even to accept that the problem will continue unless more radical steps are taken. Gil's story illustrates the fact that LEGUP throws the emphasis on to the presenter – the manager is not waving a magic wand but inviting and assisting the presenter to take constructive action for himself. Gil may want to continue with tackling his problem, in which case it is back to LEGUP to search for better ways. But if he does not then he needs to accept that the responsibility lies with him. This will help him to refrain from blaming outside sources for the restriction on his career, and he may well be ready to face the problem again at some point in the future.

Looking back at LEGUP

We have reached the end of the LEGUP process on a realistic note. This is important. While I have attempted to describe problem solving face to face in terms of what actually happens in a business situation, it is as well to be reminded that it is a great deal easier to describe management skills than it is to carry them out. When I have tackled problems 'according to the book' I have had the satisfaction of seeing the process through without faltering. But on occasions I have been conscious of letting my skills slip, or of encountering new situations for which I was not properly prepared.

I know that I am capable of deep listening, but I have caught myself failing to do it – my attention has been elsewhere, or I have not resisted the temptation to come back with an instinctive response rather than a mirror summary. Looking back at the exploration of a problem I have realized that I had omitted to use a skill which could have helped, or used it awkwardly. Sometimes I have leapt too easily at a hypothesis which turned out to be premature. I have been known to ignore my own advice by hoping that a satisfactory exploration will be enough and that the setting of goals is unnecessary. And I have accepted goals which did not stand up to the CROW criteria. It has sometimes proved easier to ignore underpinning than to arrange for it; and, on occasion, I have taken pursuit for granted.

This is not an exercise in humility but in realism. In the rush and pressures of business life perfection is rarely achieved, and we often settle for less. We have to be content with that. But there are consolations. Again and again when I have fallen short of my intentions I have been reminded – by the consequences – of the importance of the LEGUP process and the proper use of its skills. And so I have been able to test the

method both in the successful use of it, and in observing the
poor outcomes when I have not used it, or used it badly. I
made the point in the first chapter that one cause of poor
problem solving was lack of feedback. A great virtue of
LEGUP is that feedback is continuous, and so I continue to
improve. So should you.

Summary

- The Pursuit stage is an integral part of the problem
  solving process; it is important for ensuring that chosen
  goals are accomplished, and for managing the agreed
  strategy.

- One function is to provide the immediate reward for a
  goal through the manager's acknowledgement. This
  acknowledgement must be genuine and interested.
  Other functions are concerned with coaching the goal
  strategy, and analysing why goals have not been completed, so that further action can be taken.

- Managers should investigate the completion of goals
  carefully in order to make sure they have been
  properly carried through and are effective; without this
  knowledge they cannot help the presenter with the
  next stage. They also need to know when a goal has
  not been completed or attempted; presenters are not
  invariably frank about this.

- Where a number of sub-goals are involved the Pursuit
  stage is used to register the completion of an earlier
  goal, and then to provide underpinning for the following goal.

- There are a number of reasons why a goal may not
  have been completed – some are good reasons, some
  are not. The manager needs to distinguish if he is to
  help further. The seven reasons are listed on p. 184.

- The Pursuit stage shows clearly the action-centred
  nature of LEGUP. The manager has his respon-

sibilities, and so does the presenter. If when the process has been exhausted the presenter is not ready to take his responsibilities the manager cannot help him, and the consequences must be faced.

- Any management process like LEGUP must be viewed realistically. It is not infallible, and its effectiveness depends on the manager's success in using it in a business context. However, LEGUP provides continual feedback, and this is a stimulus to improvement.

14 LEGUP – a Tool for Management

Following the completed description of the LEGUP process for solving problems face to face, this chapter looks at some ways in which the LEGUP skills and process can be adapted for other management purposes. In the first section the relevance of skills to everyday management tasks is described. This is followed by the use of LEGUP with the boss – he may have a problem requiring skilled help; you may be the boss's problem; you may have a problem with which you need his help. In the third section the use of the skills and the process for groups is described; the groups may be just two people in conflict, or a small business group which is met to solve a problem.

LEGUP is an orderly, intelligent routine which incorporates a number of management skills. We would therefore expect that it could easily be adapted for use in a variety of situations beyond the face to face problems in which we have viewed it. Three of these are described in this chapter:

1 Making use of LEGUP skills for everyday management tasks.

2 Using LEGUP with your boss.

3 Using LEGUP in small groups.

LEGUP skills in everyday management

Listening

Good listening, with the reflective summaries which confirm to the speaker that his message has been understood, has its obvious application as a first step in the problem solving process. Without the relationship of trust which it builds up, the mutual and constructive exploration of the problem is unlikely to take place. But it is not a technique to soften up the presenter for a particular purpose, it is the expression of a whole attitude towards other people. A good listener is implicitly saying that the respect he has for others leads him to want to give them his full attention and to understand – as best he can – their point of view. And if he believes this, good listening simply becomes the natural way for him to listen to people. He listens to his spouse, his children and his friends in this way. And, in business, he listens to his colleagues and his staff.

The message he conveys by so doing is a powerful one. He is telling people that they are important to him; it is, in fact, a way of acknowledging them, and indicating his respect for what they have to say. Talking to a good listener is a rewarding experience: he makes you feel good, and you feel good about him. The respect he shows to you is automatically reciprocated.

In addition to this message it is obvious (though often forgotten) that the manager is much more likely to obtain and absorb information accurately. And this comes about partly because his degree of attention allows him to pick up the whole picture, uncontaminated by his own reactions; and partly because the speaker is encouraged to be more open and objective in what he has to say. Since the manager will usually have to react, either by speech or action, to what has been said, getting the best information is important.

If you have been practising good listening since you read the early chapters of this book, you will by now be agreeing with me that it is a difficult task. The difficulty does not so much lie in the method as in the self-discipline required in forcing ourselves to see things from the perspective of another. But if your practice has been consistent you will also have discovered the rewards, and these are what make it worthwhile. If you have not persisted then you may like to remind yourself of the Franklin self-organizer (p. 10); this may help you to acquire the habit of using the skill regularly.

Empathy. Empathy – the particular aspect of good listening which relates to the ability to see things from another's perspective – can also be used on its own:

> Genevieve is the corporate affairs chief of an international company. She is concerned about Daniel, a bright young executive, whose ambition sticks out like a sore thumb. Every five minutes of the day Daniel appears in Genevieve's office presenting work for her approval. And, just recently he has been hinting that he wants to be able to deal directly with the chairman, rather than always going through Genevieve. She finds these habits very irritating, and has caught herself deliberately ignoring Daniel or finding ways to put him down. She realizes she must deal with Daniel directly. But, before doing so, she obliges herself to imagine what it must be like to be him, and to have the feelings and the impulses which lead to his behaviour. When she has done this her better understanding of Daniel lessens her irritation and helps her to be more relaxed about the situation. She is able to deal with him in a much more sympathetic way, and to be more ready to find constructive ways of guiding him into more appropriate behaviour.

> Ronald, an insurance company actuary, has recently turned down an application for a large insurance policy on the grounds of the applicant's health. Today he received a memorandum from the salesman concerned which was frankly rude, and accused him of putting bureaucracy ahead of profitable business. Checking his impulse to write back in a similar vein, Ronald tried to imagine what it would be like to have worked hard to make a sale which carried considerable commission, and then to have it turned down at the last ditch for reasons which seem obscure. The note which he sends back is rightly firm, but it acknowledges the salesman's disappointment and gives a fuller explanation of the reasons.

Listening to oneself. Problem presenters are not the only people who have confused feelings and thoughts; managers do, too. We might imagine Genevieve, in the example above, coming to terms with her own feelings by trying to describe them to herself. And she obeys just the same rules: she does not try to criticize or excuse how she feels – just to be honest in her expression of it. They might sound like this:

> 'Every time I see Daniel hovering at my office door I feel haunted, I find myself turning away avoiding his eye. But I know he'll come in, and I'll find it difficult to control the irritation in my voice. I feel guilty at the same time – he's keen and his work's good; I ought to be better with him. When he asks to see the chairman with his work I try to be patient, but actually I feel insulted – that he doesn't trust me. I just don't like his pushiness. Perhaps I'm a bit scared of it. I'm certainly scared of it getting out of control – it'll reflect on me. But I can also see that Daniel is doing himself harm; far from getting on he'll get a reputation for pushiness which will damage his chances. I don't want that, but the way I'm dealing with it – or rather, not dealing with it – isn't going to help.'

Managers would often find it difficult to admit to feelings like that to another person – pride, and the need to give the impression of being in control, stand in the way. It can even be difficult to admit them to oneself. Yet just as it is true that the presenter can often only sort out, accept, and begin to deal with his feelings by articulating them, so Genevieve – and all of us – can do our jobs better by listening to ourselves as we are, and not as we would wish to be. Try it out right now: take some aspect of your managerial life where you suspect you have some strong feelings, and level with yourself. Don't worry if it sounds stupid, as long as it's as honest as you can make it. Then see, perhaps over a period of time, if it helps you to feel more relaxed about the situation, and more capable of dealing with it.

Exploration skills

Many of the powerful skills used at the Exploration stage are relevant to the general tasks of managers. A great deal of their work will be taken up in exploring and understanding situations so that the right decisions may be taken; and, as I have just described with listening, the manager may need to use the skills on himself as much as on other parties involved in the investigation. The general pattern will be similar – taking the facts as they are initially known, questioning them (creative questions), seeing their deeper meaning (interpretive summaries), looking at the feelings which surround the facts – which may be contaminating them, or which need to be taken into account, trying to turn vague thoughts into a concrete form to test their validity or relevance. Skills such as looking for patterns and inconsistencies will be relevant. Changing frames of reference ('Let's try and work out how the customer will see that benefit') will be used frequently. Identifying the assumptions which we bring to a management task, and then testing their validity, will often change the whole nature of a decision. The formation of hypotheses – tentative at first but gradually being confirmed by testing – will generally be used in order to find the best fit leading to appropriate action.

Goal setting skills

Management by Objectives (MBO) is a popular approach to management. It just seems commonsense to agree clear and reasonable objectives with staff, and then to measure the results by agreed criteria. Management knows what to expect, staff know what is expected of them – and both have the satisfaction of knowing when the task is well done. But it isn't always like that in practice. The goal setting skills which I have described are not particularly difficult to use, but you do need to know about them, and you do need to be practised in the techniques. In their absence attempts at MBO are frustrating for both parties and, in the end, may turn out to be counterproductive. The old informal methods may not have seemed very modern or scientific, but they worked reasonably well. Poorly conducted MBO is neither one thing nor the other. But the CROW principles, properly mastered, perhaps through practice at solving problems face to face, can be employed directly in an MBO system in order to make it a truly effective management tool. It can be used as a general planning technique, or to direct a specific project. And of course good goal setting is the key to staff annual assessments and career development interviews.

Other skills

The need for Underpinning follows logically when any goals are being set, and a proper programme of Pursuit will be essential. A reliable sign of poor goal setting is that Pursuit is not carried out effectively and enthusiastically by either party. If the goals failed in being concrete, realistic, observable and worthwhile there is little satisfaction in checking on success. It either won't have occurred, or there will be no objective way of measuring it. And, of course, the failure to pursue removes an opportunity for establishing at an early stage whether and why goals are going wrong, with the possibility of corrective action in good time.

LEGUP and your boss

In this book I have discussed problem solving principally in terms of a manager dealing with a subordinate or with peers. But most of us are somewhere on the hierarchical ladder, with a boss above as well as staff below; and even chief executive officers are likely to have a board to answer to. Problems with bosses take two main forms: a problem which the boss presents and with which he wants help; and a situation in which *we* are the problem presenter, either because we have a difficulty to raise with the boss or because he has a difficulty with some aspect of our performance. The LEGUP method, suitably adapted, can be used for either.

The boss has a problem

In an ideal world the process of LEGUP could be used without changing a word to assist our boss to solve a problem. In practice the way the methods are used and the atmosphere in which the process is conducted is likely to alter. The degree of alteration will vary according to the relationship, and each manager must decide this for himself.

> When Craig is carrying out problem solving with his staff he is used to introducing the subject of goal setting quite firmly, for instance: 'OK, now we seem to have got the nature of the problem clear, it's important that we set quite specific goals to be achieved in order to put it right.' Finding himself in a similar position with his boss it seems more tactful to say: 'I hope that's helped to clarify the situation for you. But it does look as if you're going to have to pull off some specific things if you're going to make it come out right. Would it help you if we discussed some rather clear goals for you to accomplish?

The dividing line between tact and sycophancy is not always easy to find. Perhaps a good criterion is what we would expect of our own subordinates – making due allowance for any particular quirks in our boss's character.

Do not underestimate how valuable you can be to a boss in helping him to solve a problem. His need to have someone to help him to articulate his difficulties, to explore them, and to establish a sensible strategy for putting things right, is as great for him as anyone else. But – particularly if he is the top man – he may have less opportunity than others to get skilled assistance. And there is another benefit: the example of good problem solving which you demonstrate may well increase your boss's skills – and you could be the next beneficiary!

You are the boss's problem

Yes, it can happen. It may be a straightforward occasion when the boss wants you to achieve some different objective or behave in a different kind of way. Or he may be mildly or strongly dissatisfied with some aspect of your work. The application of LEGUP needs some simple adaptation here because it is not clear who is managing the process, and therefore what roles the participants should be playing. Let's take an example:

Gudgeon has asked to see you. He has on his desk a letter from a large customer complaining that the last order delivered was faulty in certain respects. This, the customer claims, is the second time it has happened and he will place no more orders unless Gudgeon give his personal assurance that there will be no further problems. Gudgeon is not happy. And he is not happy with you in particular.

A number of thoughts spring to your mind: it's not really your responsibility; that particular customer would complain about the seating arrangements in Heaven; you haven't enough staff to cope. But remembering the Listening stage, you suppress all of these so that you can absorb Gudgeon's feelings and thoughts about the situation, and reflect back to him so that he knows you have heard. In this way you relieve the tension of the situation. Gudgeon wants you to know he is angry, or worried, or concerned, and you confirm that you have taken in his feelings. You have been neither defensive nor apologetic, and, in this way, you are turning a confrontation into an objective problem which needs both your minds to solve. It may even be that, after this, Gudgeon re-states himself, realizing that his initial remarks were stronger than they need have been to make his point.

In the Exploration stage you invite him to examine with you the nature of the problem in order to establish what has gone wrong, what has contributed to it, and what has to be put right. Your contribution to the problem should be acknowledged quite objectively, but, by the same token, other contributions must also be considered as the hypotheses are reviewed. It turns out that in this case the customer's specifications were not clear, and his requirements were misunderstood by your department. You take personal responsibility for not having queried the specifications at the beginning, particularly since this customer was a known complainer. However, you were in the United States at the time and you have no experienced deputy since the company has not permitted you to recruit one. There is no need for accusations or counteraccusations at this stage, and if your boss's stronger feelings recur they should be listened to and reflected before moving the conversation back to a discussion of the problem.

The conclusion you reach mutually is that this customer, and a short list of similarly difficult people, will in future have their orders vetted by you personally. In your absence your boss will act for you; and, if the situation arises frequently, he will permit you to recruit a deputy at the appropriate level. He will reply to the aggrieved customer immediately, and you will take an early opportunity to visit him in order to develop a better line of communication. Thus goals will be set, and the underpinning required will be provided. And you will suggest, if your boss doesn't, a pursuit time when both of you will review the action taken and its effectiveness.

The strategy here is straightforward. You are aiming to turn a situation where strong feelings and concerns (perhaps quite understandable) are turning a business problem into a blame game which will only interfere with finding the best remedy. As in any other problem solving situation you do not try to stifle the feelings, nor judge them. On the contrary, you help them to be expressed and recognize them through reflection. Once in the open they can be dealt with more readily, and given their due place within the problem. But your objective, and – at least, ultimately – your boss's objective, is the discovery and implementation of the best solution.

Presenting a problem to your boss

Naturally you will have, over a period of time, a variety of problems which you would want your boss to solve, or at least assist with the solution. Sadly, he is not familiar with LEGUP. What do you do?

Barbara has lost three key members of staff during the last six months. She is concerned about her ability to meet her department's objectives. And she is also wondering why staff are leaving – is it something she's doing, or the company's employment policies, or what? Her boss used to run her department until his promotion, and she thinks his experience will help her to sort things out. But she hardly has time to state the outline of the problem before he interrupts to say that he has been watching the situation, and is even more concerned than she is. Fortunately his experience gives him the answers so he does not have to pause for Barbara to react before giving her a three-point plan for correcting matters. Finally he ushers Barbara out of his office with the avuncular smile of a man who knows he has done a good job.

You may be able to guess how Barbara is feeling now. And there is no neat way in which LEGUP can be transferred by osmosis or even by hitting someone over the head with a copy of this book. Theologians use the term 'invincible ignorance', and, if you come across it, recognize it and cut your losses. However, with patience some situations can be rescued. Unless you have the sort of relationship with your boss which allows you to suggest to him that he might try listening and exploring first, you have to seek an opportunity in which you can demonstrate by example. And listening is usually the best point to start:

> Two days later Barbara goes in to see her boss again. She tells him she has been thinking about his three-point plan, but it's so important to her that she wants to make sure she has understood fully. He is pleased by this thought, and is happy to let her reflect to him what she believes she heard. He basically confirms her understanding but, hearing her summary, feels he should develop some of the points further. Barbara continues to reflect, and the conversation relaxes so that Barbara is able to present her worries more fully. Her boss has, apparently, never had a worry about such matters and his sense of superiority enables him to be more objective. He even listens a little. Barbara is able to merge the conversation gradually into exploration – bringing in, incidentally, a number of factors which the three-point plan did not address. Her boss begins to see that the situation is more complex than he had at first imagined, and he starts to help her explore. Once they have agreed on the core of the problem and what has to change, Barbara says she finds it easier to work with concrete goals, and asks him to help her establish these. Underpinning and pursuit follow a similar course.

Barbara's situation has worked out better than she might have expected. At least she has had a degree of useful help.

And she may have been lucky: her boss could easily have
been insensitive to her attempts, and she would still have got
nowhere. Nevertheless she followed the best available
strategy – to try with some tact to guide the discussion into a
LEGUP form. If she gets nothing else out of it Barbara will
now have an even stronger motivation to use LEGUP with
her own staff.

Using LEGUP with small groups

Two people in conflict

You may remember the story of John Serbo, the managing
director who had two divisional managers given to bickering
with each other over responsibilities and demarcation (p.
169). This kind of difficulty can appear at all levels in an
organization, and is usually very counterproductive. When
the two people concerned are not able to sort themselves
out, even with encouragement, a third party who can provide them with a framework for tackling the differences, and
who can coach them through the problem solving process,
acting as a kind of umpire, can be invaluable. Let's follow
the story through:

> Before John Serbo gets Perry and Martin together in the same
> room he seeks an opportunity to talk to each of them separately.
> This is easy to arrange with Perry because he has raised the
> problem quite frequently with John, and he welcomes a full
> discussion. John starts by using good listening, and takes in all
> Perry's frustrations and sense of strain. He listens to the criti-
> cisms of Martin, reflecting but not commenting. When he has
> the full picture from Perry's viewpoint they start to explore using
> several of the skills described, and making good use of frames
> of reference which enable Perry to gain some insight into
> Martin's perspective. Perry believes the difficulties are none of
> his making, but he does accept that a bad pattern has been set
> up, and that he is contributing to it.
>
> The interview with Martin is more difficult. Martin doesn't

believe (or doesn't wish to believe) that there is a problem, and is therefore reluctant to talk about it. John, however, makes it clear that, even if the problem is only in Perry's mind, it has to be dealt with. Martin responds to this with a number of criticisms of Perry, to which John listens carefully. Martin relaxes a little, and they explore the problem together – although it is hard to get Martin to look at the situation from any point of view other than his own. At this stage John finds himself leaning towards Perry's side. At least he appears to be open to change. But he checks this feeling, recognizing that any partiality would disqualify him from being helpful.

He calls them both in together, and invites them to express the situation as they see it. Initially they are both hesitant, and John has to help the dialogue by reminding them of some their previous remarks. As the conversation starts to develop John makes sure that the whole picture, as previously given to him, is brought into the open. He knows that they will not find it easy to be frank when they are eyeball to eyeball, but frankness is essential. However his presence as umpire is reassuring, and his reflection and summarizing of what is being said help the discussion of feelings and experiences to be reasonably objective. Occasionally he has to check interruptions so that points can be made properly, and to control too much repetition. At the right moment he summarizes, checks that he has the correct picture, and moves them into exploration. He is able to bring into this stage some of the ideas which they have expressed in the earlier interviews and, between them, they start to make some sense of the problem.

It seems that neither feels any fundamental ill will; in fact it is the respect they have for each other's abilities which is contributing to their sense of being threatened. They are also able to realize that their business futures are likely to be improved by pooling their strengths in the company's interests rather than wasting it in disputes. Once they have accepted this they feel free to look at the demarcation problems, and to decide on lines of responsibility. John Serbo realizes that he, too, has contributed to the problem by failing to clarify aspects of their jobs. He must now do this, and also be ready to give a ruling on any points where Perry and Martin cannot agree. Thus they are jointly able to set goals for change, with the appropriate underpinning; and John sets up the next meeting to evaluate their progress.

Naturally the course of any dispute will vary with its nature, and with the personalities of the participants. But you will see from this example that the basic LEGUP process is being used, although some extra dimensions are present. Serbo has used the method of the individual interview in order to obtain a fuller initial picture. This helps him with his real objective: to get Perry and Martin to act as joint problem solvers. To do this they have to listen and understand, and then work their way through exploration and the later stages. He acts as teacher, coach and conductor of the process – although, as sometimes occurs in face to face problems, it turns out in this instance that he is also a participant, ending up with goals of his own.

Working with a group

The whole matter of effective group leadership requires a book to itself. In this section I propose only to talk about some ways in which LEGUP skills can make a particular contribution to the process.

Groups are sometimes set up specifically for problem solving, and they will in any event often find themselves in this role. Two points are relevant here: there are bound to be different points of view in a group – otherwise there's little sense in having one, and participants are likely to have different experience and responsibilities. This suggests that some of the LEGUP skills will be appropriate in order to achieve constructive harmony. Secondly, if the object of the group is to solve a problem effectively then it is likely that listening, exploring, goal setting, underpinning, and pursuit will be components of the process.

Constructive harmony. Musical harmony involves not everyone playing the same note, but the different notes blending to achieve the right sound. This suggests that the musicians should understand what their fellows are doing, and the parts which individually and collectively are con-

tributing to the whole effect. It will also be helpful to have a
conductor (who does not play an instrument himself) or a
leader (who both plays and leads). This analogy may help us
to see the contribution which LEGUP skills can make. For
instance the skills of listening and frame of reference changing will be important.

> Don has met with his area sales managers to discuss the problem
> they are having with recruiting high quality salesmen. The man-
> agers have been worried about this for a long time and, when the
> topic is opened, everyone has a view. Unfortunately the priority is
> to communicate this view and not to listen to anyone else, except
> to shoot down their particular theory. Don immediately exerts his
> authority to prevent interruptions, listens carefully to what is
> being said, and reflects. He will not permit a new speaker until
> the previous one has been heard. At this early stage he discour-
> ages any comment on the different ideas until all the managers
> have had a chance to say what they think. Then he summarizes
> the ideas, suggesting that behind the superficial differences the
> group is suggesting two basic approaches to the problem.
>
> As they move into exploration, they quickly return to criticizing
> each other's ideas. But Don insists that before they do so, they say
> what they understand the idea to be – as their colleague has
> expressed it. In this way he ensures that the ideas have been
> understood and that some progress has been made towards
> recognizing the proposer's frame of reference before the criti-
> cism takes place. They have some difficulty with this, and Don
> decides that a 'lightning lesson' is needed (p. 174). He *Explains*
> how this ensures that the suggestion has been properly appreci-
> ated, and that what is being criticized is what was actually
> suggested. He *Demonstrates* what he means by modelling an
> example based on an actual suggestion. He requires the group to
> *Practise* the method as they continue their discussion; and he
> *Reviews* their performance by inviting the original speaker to
> say whether or not their critic has reflected accurately.

It may seem cumbersome to halt the process of the group in
order to get them to work with the best skills. One could
imagine the participants being thoroughly distracted from
their task by learning to do things in a new way. But the group

which appears in this example is likely to meet together
frequently, and it is certainly worth the time invested to get
them into the habit of constructive harmony through good
listening and reflecting. In practice the group quickly learns
these standards, and begins to police itself by pulling up
transgressors. Additionally the example of listening, continuously given by the manager, is quickly adopted through
imitation. In fact the leader is actually training the group to
work well, and the use of other skills will contribute to this
process. Even a group which comes together for only one
occasion will find itself working better if the manager is
giving examples of good group behaviour.

Using the other skills. The other skills of the LEGUP process
should be used when appropriate. Here are a few examples:

> Don uses creative questioning to help the group explore the
> suggested ideas more deeply.
>   He asks them to look at the fact that each time they have had a
> big recruiting effort results have improved temporarily but
> swiftly fallen back. Is there a pattern here, he asks.
>   The group speaks about the importance of selecting sales-
> men with good basic education. Don asks them to consider
> whether this view is inconsistent with the records, which show
> that the educational standards are not high.
>   New salesmen have usually had previous experience in the
> industry. We make the assumption, says Don, that this is neces-
> sary; and he suggests that the group should test whether this
> assumption really holds.
>   He helps the group to avoid vague generalizations by inviting
> them to give concrete examples of what they mean.
>   Someone suggests that the problem lies more in the retention
> of existing salesmen than in the recruitment of new ones. Don
> invites the group into a new frame of reference by asking them
> to say how the career looks from the salesman's point of view.
>   Another suggestion is that the company should invest more
> money in its recruitment programme. Don asks the group to test
> the consequences of this by measuring the suggested invest-
> ment against the likely increased revenue.

You will have observed that the skills in these examples come directly from Chapters 6 and 7, where they are described under the Exploration stage. The other skills described can be used with equal effect – indeed it is possible to use most of the methods more directly and challengingly with a group since it is likely to have greater resilience than an individual. But this only applies to the group as a whole – you should be careful with the individual members of the group who, being in front of their peers, are more exposed. This is particularly important in the matter of exploring feelings, which should be reserved for face to face discussion until you know the group and its members very well.

Using the LEGUP process with the group. Problem solving groups need to go through just the same stages as problem solving individuals and therefore the LEGUP process, with minor adaptations, is directly applicable. We have already looked at the way the Listening stage might be handled: the thoughts, the feelings, the information are taken in by the group, and summarized so that they may be explored. The Exploration stage takes its normal course of examining this material so that the core of the the problem may be discovered, and who or what has to be changed may be identified. And hypotheses will be put forward for examination until the best fit is established. Goal setting is just as important for a group as for an individual, and clear assignment of responsibility will be essential. Underpinning and Pursuit will have parallel functions to those in a face to face situation.

In the example above Don, the manager, has assumed the role of the conductor of the 'orchestra'; that is, he has enabled the group to work effectively but he has not made a contribution himself. He could have taken the additional role of leader of the orchestra as well – both conducting and playing. In this way his own experience and suggestions would have been at the disposal of the group. But caution is needed here: just as the presenter in the face to face problem is happy to let the manager do his work for him so the group may be inclined to take Don's suggestions without critical examination. He must train them to discuss his views as freely as they discuss the views of their colleagues; and he may be wise to hold back on expressing himself until other views have been canvassed.

In doing so he does not abrogate his management responsibilities, and he can set these as he chooses. He may want the group to solve the problem themselves, and be prepared to stand by their conclusions. He may want to do this, but to keep their conclusions within defined limits. Or he may want to reserve the right to accept or reject their conclusions. The group needs to know where he stands on this, although it may be clear from his habitual behaviour. But even the most common position – reserving the right to final decisions – requires that the group is enabled to work freely, and that the manager should be strongly influenced by its conclusions, which will only be rejected in extreme cases. Otherwise there is little sense in using a group, and the group itself will quickly learn to perform poorly.

Summary

LEGUP skills in everyday management

- Good listening is more than a technique, it is an expression of an attitude of respect towards people. It should be employed constantly, thus improving staff motivation as well as ensuring that good information is communicated.

- Empathy, or the ability to see the situation from the viewpoint of another person, should be cultivated and used wherever appropriate. It will help the manager to respond to others in a useful way.

- A manager should not neglect to listen to himself. In this way he can realize his own attitudes and feelings, and thus learn to use them constructively.

- Many of the skills of the Exploration stage will be useful to the manager in dealing with other problems or decisions than those presented to him face to face.

- The skills of the Goal setting stage (remember CROW) will be applicable whenever management by objectives, annual appraisal and similar management methods are used. Similarly, Underpinning and Pursuit will often be needed for general management tasks.

LEGUP and your boss

- When your boss needs help with a problem the LEGUP method should be used. However a degree of tact and sensitivity should be used in employing the method.

- If the boss has a problem with you, you should still attempt to steer the dialogue into a LEGUP form, and to use the appropriate skills. This will help the discussion to address the problem objectively, while giving full weight to any feelings your boss may have about you or the situation.

- If you have a problem with which you require the boss's help, you are more likely to receive this effectively if he can be induced to use the LEGUP form. This is not always easy with an unskilled boss, but giving him a model of good listening may be the best way to start.

Using LEGUP with small groups

- LEGUP is useful for resolving differences between two people; in this case the participants are being helped to work through the process together. Since all the difficulties need to be expressed it may help if the manager has listened to them, and done some initial exploration, with each participant on his own, first.

- In ordinary business groups which meet to solve problems the skills of LEGUP can be used successfully to enable the group to pool its different resources in constructive harmony. The manager should be ready to teach the group to use the skills, and this will prove a good investment of time in the long run.

- The LEGUP process can be used, with very little

adaptation, as a framework for group problem solving. The manager must make his role, and how he intends to exercise his authority, clear to the group.

Select Bibliography

Buzan, Tony, *Use Your Head*, BBC Publications, 1974.
This book, presented originally as a television series, is packed with practical skills invaluable to managers. Recommended here especially for paper and pencil work.

Drucker, Peter, *People and Performance*, Heinemann, 1977.
Those who have not read Drucker before will find this a good introduction to him; it will leave you in no doubt about the importance and responsibilities of managers today.

Egan, Gerard, *The Skilled Helper*, Wadsworth Publishing, Belmont, California, 1975.
See Preface for reference to Egan.

Eysenck, H.J., *You and Neurosis*, Fontana/Collins, 1977.
You don't need to be neurotic to benefit from this description of the unconscious influences on human behaviour. Hardheaded and factual.

Franklin, Benjamin (edited Lemisch), *The Autobiography and Other Writings*, The New English Library, 1961.
Contains Franklin's own account of the 'Self Organizer'. But the other selections are worth reading too.

Likert, Rensis, *New Patterns of Management*, McGraw-Hill, 1961.
An impressive, and well documented, account of management by consent.

Nierenberg, G.I. and Colero, H.H., *How to Read a Person like a Book*, Hawthorne, 1971.

Of the many works about non-verbal communication I have found this the most practical to use. The line drawings are excellent.

Priestley, Philip (and others), *Social Skills and Personal Problem Solving*, Tavistock, 1978.

This handbook of methods was designed for social work rather than management. But it contains many useful and adaptable ideas.

Rogers, Carl, *On Becoming a Person*, Constable, 1967.

This is the classic work on human maturity and fulfilment, and provides an excellent background to listening. A warning: this book can change your life.

Sharpe, R. and Lewis, D., *The Success Factor*, Pan, 1977.

This is a self-improvement book, soundly based in behavioural science. Working through it will not only be valuable in its own right, it will teach you a great deal about helping others – particularly in matters of goal and reward.

Sydney, Elizabeth (and others), *Skills with People, A Guide for Managers*, Hutchinson, 1973.

Its title describes it accurately.

Vroom, V.H. and Deci, E.L. (editors), *Management and Motivation*, Penguin, 1970.

This is a book of readings which contains the essence of many of the leading modern writers on motivation. It stimulates ideas and gives direction for further reading.